Josh + Britta,

We cherish your partnership in this business - ministry (ministry)!

Our goal is that everyone involved grows closer to Jesus through our efforts!

This book has made a lot of sense for me + helps confirm why we believe. Hopefully it will help you as well & may serve as a discussion platform for conversations among the precious (prescious) people God brings to the Whitecap family!

Neal / Dad

Jeany / mom

REFLECTIONS ON THE EXISTENCE of GOD

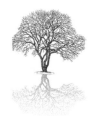

Reflections on the Existence of God

A SERIES OF ESSAYS

RICHARD E.
SIMMONS III

Reflections on the Existence of God

Union Hill is the book publishing imprint of The Center for
Executive Leadership, a 501(c)3 nonprofit organization.

Union Hill Publishing
200 Union Hill Drive, Suite 200
Birmingham, AL 35209

www.richardesimmons3.com

5 6 7 8 9 10

Printed in the United States of America

To Billy Wood.
Without his influential friendship,
this book may never have been written.

Also by

Richard E. Simmons III

THE REASON FOR LIFE
Why Did God Put Me Here?

THE POWER OF A HUMBLE LIFE
Quiet Strength in an Age of Arrogance

WISDOM
Life's Great Treasure

SEX AT FIRST SIGHT
Understanding the Modern Hookup Culture

A LIFE OF EXCELLENCE
Wisdom for Effective Living

THE TRUE MEASURE OF A MAN
How Perceptions of Success,
Achievement & Recognition Fail Men in Difficult Times

RELIABLE TRUTH
The Validity of the Bible in an Age of Skepticism

SAFE PASSAGE
Thinking Clearly About Life & Death

REMEMBERING THE FORGOTTEN GOD
The Search for Truth in the Modern World

Table of Contents

Preface

THE TERM "New Atheists" was coined back in 2006 by the journalist Gary Wolf, as he was describing the positions promoted by some of the most outspoken and popular atheists of the twenty-first century. They all viewed religion as nothing more than superstition. The four most prominent people in this group were Sam Harris, Richard Dawkins, Christopher Hitchens (now deceased), and Daniel Dennett. They have been referred to as "The Four Horsemen" of atheism.

One of "The Four Horsemen," Sam Harris, a best-selling author, penned some words that reflect the purpose of this book. Recognizing that atheism and Christianity compete on the same playing field, he remarked:

> "So let us be honest with ourselves; in the fullness of time, one side is going to really win this argument, and the other side is really going to lose."[1]

Harris is right.

THIS BOOK is a series of short essays seeking to answer life's most enduring question: Does God exist? I have attempted to craft a book that is well researched (I have been conducting this research for over 30 years) but also easy to read and understand. Each essay can be read in less than 10 minutes.

I draw my research from the great atheist thinkers over the ages—from philosophers Friedrich Nietzsche, Jean-Paul Sartre, Albert Camus, and Bertrand Russell to scientists like Charles Darwin, Richard Dawkins, and Daniel Dennett. On the theistic perspective, I look to a number of great thinkers as well, most who subscribe to a Judeo-Christian worldview. This is because this particular worldview has provided the foundation for the rise of Western civilization.

The question of God's existence, in my opinion, is the most significant issue in all of life. As renowned French philosopher and mathematician Blaise Pascal said, you're betting your eternal destiny that you are right.

Armand Nicholi was a clinical professor of psychiatry at Harvard Medical School and author of one of my favorite books, *The Question of God.* The book is based on a course he taught at Harvard's undergraduate school. In the course he compares the lives and beliefs of Sigmund Freud, the atheist, with C.S. Lewis, the Christian. It is a fascinating read. In the prologue of the book, Nicholi writes some interesting words contrasting these two men's views on the existence of God. He says:

> "Are these worldviews merely philosophical speculations with no right or wrong answer? No. One of them begins with the basic premise that God does not exist, the other with the premise that He does. They are, therefore, mutually exclusive—if one is right, the other must be wrong. Does it really make any difference to know which one is which? Both Freud and Lewis thought so. They spent a good portion of their lives exploring these issues, repeatedly asking the question 'Is it true?'"[2]

Is what I believe true? I cannot think of anything more tragic than to live my life with a false view of reality. A false view of the existence of God.

Lewis and Freud clearly believed this is the most important issue in all of life. Lewis said, "Here is a door behind which, according to some people, the secret of the universe is waiting for you. Either that is true or it isn't." Nicholi then says:

> "[If Lewis is wrong] the only alternative is to follow Freud's advice to grow up and face the harsh reality that we are alone in the universe. He says we may find less consolation, but the truth, harsh as it is, will ultimately set us free from false hopes and unrealistic expectations. But if the spiritual worldview is true, then all other truth fades in significance. Nothing has more profound and more far-reaching implications for our lives."[3]

As you read through these essays, I would remind you that atheism and theism are alternative belief systems that offer radically different views. They are not just two separate views of life; they are opposing mutually exclusive views, delivering opposite conclusions about the meaning of life and our existence as human beings. A person who is seriously searching for an answer to the question of God's existence must take time to understand fully the logical conclusions derived from both theism and atheism. Ultimately, the belief which is true will be consistent with the real world and the one which is untrue will present a view of life that is not in harmony with reality.

In the end it is important to know whether God exists or He does not exist. There is no third option. What I am seeking to do in this book is to determine which of these beliefs is true and which one is not.

1.

Introductory Essays

"The best atheists agree with the best defenders of faith [in God] on one crucial point: that choice to believe or disbelieve is existentially the most important choice of all. It shapes one's whole understanding of human life and purpose, because it is a choice that each must make for him or herself."

—ADAM KIRSCH

1.1

Our Perception of Reality

A NUMBER of years ago, *Encyclopedia Britannica* published a 55-volume series entitled *The Great Books of the Western World.* This series presented the most important ideas that scholars and intellectuals have considered and investigated over the course of recorded history. The longest essay was on God.

When noted philosopher, author, and co-editor of the series, Mortimer Adler, was asked the reason behind this, he replied, "It is because more consequences for life follow from that one issue than from any other."[4]

I believe Dr. Adler's assessment is spot on. The major issues of life are understood with the greatest clarity only after the question of God's existence is placed in its proper context.

Everyone has a certain perspective on how life works. It is the lens through which we see life. It is what most people call a "worldview." When we are born, we begin to try and understand how life works. Over time, we formulate a philosophy of life, a worldview, and this worldview influences how we see ourselves, how we relate to others, and how we live our lives.

Armand Nicholi, the Harvard psychiatrist I mentioned in the preface, and the author of *The Question of God* says that our worldview informs our personal, social, and political lives. It helps us understand our purpose. Further, he said that our worldview determines our ethics, our values, and our capacity for happiness. It helps us answer the big questions of life: How did I get here? How am I to live? Where do I find meaning in life? What is my ultimate destiny? Basically, Nicholi is telling us that our worldview is more telling than perhaps any other aspect of our lives.[5]

Another way to understand our worldview is to see it as a map, a mental map that helps navigate life effectively. As author Nancy Pearcey says, "…we need some creed to live by; some map by which we chart our course." This is worldview.[6]

In forming our worldviews, Dr. Nicholi says that we make one of two assumptions about life. The first is that we live in a godless universe; we are a product of nature that has evolved over time. This is a secular worldview that emphasizes scientific knowledge and its motto is "What do science and nature have to say?"

The second assumption is that there is a supernatural intelligence who gives the universe order and life meaning. This is a spiritual worldview that is rooted in Biblical revelations. It places emphasis on spiritual truth and wisdom and its motto is: "What does God have to say about this?"[7]

I have concluded that every person has an opinion on God and spiritual reality, even if it is a belief that He is non-existent. We all have a faith view of reality and it trickles down into our lives and influences the choices we make.

Author Tim Keller says:

> "How we relate to God is the foundation of our thinking, because it determines the way we view the world. Whether you believe God exists or not, this belief is the foundation in which all of your reasoning proceeds. For instance, if you do not believe that God exists, it is a belief taken by faith and it becomes your faith view of reality. Whether you realize it or not, all your reasoning proceeds from this belief. You end up screening out all that does not fit with this view of life."[8]

Your worldview will ultimately explain where life originated, what life means, and what we are supposed to be doing with the years we are given. What I hope to accomplish in this book comes from the words of English mathematician John Lennox who says:

> "What divides us is not science . . . but our worldviews. No one wants to base their life on a delusion, but which is the delusion? Christianity or atheism?"[9]

1.2

Discovering What Is True

WE ARE seeking to discover what is true about God, but we must remember that truth is discovered and not invented. It is discovered by examining the available evidence that enables us to come to a rational conclusion. If something is supported by evidence, it is worth believing.

William Kingdon Clifford was a philosopher who lived in England more than 150 years ago. He was not very well known because his life was cut short at age 33. His recently discovered essay entitled "The Ethics of Belief" is receiving a great deal of attention.

In this essay, written in 1877, Clifford says that it is a moral obligation to believe responsibly. We must base our beliefs on sufficient evidence that we have diligently investigated. He believed this to be of such great importance because beliefs influence one's actions. They are foundational to life.

In commenting on this essay, journalist Francisco Mejia Uribe contends that Clifford is on to something because when we believe something, the stakes are high. Every single belief has the capacity to be truly consequential, particularly if the belief is in error and involves the most significant issues of life.[10]

This has caused me to wonder how many people examine the evidence on the existence of God before they come to belief. How many of them believe responsibly? I often think people make their decisions about spiritual reality based on subjective preferences. It reminds me of Pascal's observation that most people invariably arrive at their beliefs not on the basis of proof (evidence) but on the basis of what they find to be attractive to them. It is quite clear, however, that truth is not a matter of subjective taste but that which is based on objective evidence.

I might add that this tendency of not believing responsibly is true of atheists ***and*** Christians. In both cases, they cannot give a good explanation of the position they have taken; they cannot explain the evidence that has led them to belief.

This reminds me of Sir Hector Hetherington, who, for 25 years, was the Principal (what Americans call President) of the prestigious University of Glasgow in Scotland. He had this to say about our search for spiritual truth:

> "There are issues on which it is impossible to be neutral. These issues strike right down to the roots of man's existence. And while it is right that we should examine the evidence, and make sure that we have all the evidence, it is equally right that we ourselves should be accessible to the evidence. We cannot live a full life without knowing exactly where we stand regarding these fundamental issues of life and destiny." [11]

Do we not care about what is true? Are we afraid to look reality in the eye because it may take us in a direction we don't want to go? I believe this is one of the great flaws in our human character. We stubbornly hold on to our beliefs because they generally reflect how we want life to be rather than how life actually is. For this reason, evidence does not seem to matter.

A great example of this is Dr. Francis Collins. Many consider Dr. Collins to be one of the most effective and ground-breaking scientists in the world. Collins graduated with a degree in chemistry from the University of Virginia. He earned his PhD in chemistry at Yale and then decided, for good measure, he would go to medical school at the University of North Carolina. From there, he returned to Yale and later, the University of Michigan.

He is most noted for having been chosen to chair the Human Genome Project where, in 2003, he led an international collaboration of two thousand scientists in sequencing the human genome. More recently, he was appointed by President Obama to be the Director of the National Institutes of Health. Clearly, he is a prominent scientist, but what is perhaps even more interesting is his spiritual journey.

He began this journey as an atheist. In his third year of medical school, while he was working in the hospital, he was attending a woman who had exhausted her options for treatment. She suffered from a heart condition and was going to die soon. Collins was moved by this kind and faithful woman. She had a strong faith, and she shared it with him. She said, "You know, I'm ready to go. Don't worry about me."

And then she said, "Dr. Collins, you've been so kind to listen to me and care for me and listen to me share with you about my faith. Tell me about your faith. Tell me what you believe." Collins later wrote:

> "Nobody had ever asked me that question before, not like that, not in such a simple, sincere way. I realized I didn't know the answer. I felt uneasy. I could feel my face flushing. I wanted to get out of there. The ice was cracking under my feet. All of a sudden, by this simple question, everything was a muddle."[12]

Collins began to wonder if he was an atheist because he had chosen the position of reason or because it was the answer he wanted. Finally, it came to him:

> "As a scientist, I had always insisted on collecting rigorous data before drawing a conclusion. And yet, in matters of faith, I had never collected any data at all. I didn't know what I had rejected. So, I decided that I should be a little better grounded in my atheism. I better find out what this is all about. So, I challenged a patient of mine who was a

> Methodist minister. And, after listening to my questions and realizing that I was not dealing with a very full deck of information, he suggested that I read the Gospel of John, which I did…I found the scripture to be interesting, puzzling, and not at all what I had thought faith was about… then I began to read C.S. Lewis and realized there was a great depth of thinking and reasoning that could be applied to the question of God."[13]

Lewis convinced him that reason and faith go hand in hand, though faith has the added component of revelation—the Bible. Collins had previously believed that Jesus and the stories of the Bible were nothing more than mere myths. Again, as he studied the historical evidence, he was stunned at how well documented and how historically accurate the Bible is. He also saw a surprising fidelity of the transmission of the manuscripts that were passed down over the centuries. And, over time, Francis Collins, based on the accumulation of the evidence that he observed, concluded that God exists, and that Jesus is the Son of God. He also concluded that most of the religious skeptics that he knew and that he meets today are just like he was. That is to say, they didn't want to think about these things and never looked at any evidence, never drawing conclusions from the real evidence that was available.

This is what Dr. Dallas Willard, former professor of philosophy at the University of Southern California, believed was a major problem with individuals who considered themselves to be agnostic or atheist. Willard found that so many of the students and scholars he encountered on campus and in the world were guilty of what he called "irresponsible disbelief." These bright men and women would often choose to disbelieve in something without any significant commitment to an investigation of that disbelief by way of sound reasoning and careful examination of the evidence.[14]

Over 40 years ago, I read the wonderful book *A Severe Mercy*, by Sheldon Vanauken. The book details his long spiritual journey as an agnostic. Though he lived in different places in the world, he somehow struck up a long-distance friendship with C.S. Lewis. Much of the book is an exchange of letters between the two of them. Vanauken was seeking to get answers to the spiritual questions that troubled him the most. Lewis's answers provided the evidence that he needed to finally make a personal decision.

After coming to the conclusion that God exists and that Jesus was the Son of God, Vanauken was able to look back on his life and realize that he had contempt towards Christianity, but it was a contempt against something he realized he knew nothing about. He realized, like Francis Collins, that most of the people who reject Christianity know almost nothing of what they are rejecting.

This book lays out, in short essays, much of the evidence for the existence of God that is available. We should seek to take the evidence offered and use it to make reasonable conclusions. What you will find is, as the evidence accumulates, it enables us to come to confident conclusions about God. Who He is. And, that He truly is.

1.3

Follow the Truth Wherever It Leads

PHILOSOPHER DOUGLAS Groothuis made this observation about the truth:

> "Truth is a daunting, difficult thing, it is also the greatest thing in the world. Yet we are chronically ambivalent toward it. We seek it…and we fear it. Our better side wants to pursue truth wherever it leads; our darker side balks when the truth begins to lead us anywhere we do not want to go."[15]

This is particularly true as it relates to the human search for God. The evidence for God is really of little use if a person does not want Him in his or her life.

In this essay, I want to consider the lives of Antony Flew and C.S. Lewis and their journey from atheism to theism. Both men were members of The Oxford Socratic Club, a student-led organization that was dedicated to providing an open forum for the discussion of the intellectual issues connected with religion and specifically Christianity. The club clearly had an impact on these intellectual giants who spent over a decade together adhering to the practice of Socrates—following the argument wherever it led. The members were committed to following the truth of all arguments, even if it led them in a direction that they did not want to go.

MOST PEOPLE do not know that British philosopher Antony Flew was one of the most celebrated atheists of the last 50 years. For five decades, he launched an aggressive attack on the existence of God. And then, in 2007, he stunned the world by announcing that he had changed his mind. He laid out his reasoning in his book *There Is a God: How the World's Most Notorious Atheist Changed His Mind.* In the book he states:

> "I now believe that the universe was brought into existence by an infinite intelligence. I believe that this universe's intricate laws manifest what scientists have called the Mind of God. I believe that life and reproduction originate in a divine Source. Why do I believe this, given that I expounded and defended atheism for more than half a century? The short answer is this: This is the world picture, as I see it, that has emerged from modern science."[16]

At a symposium at New York University, Flew shared some controversial thoughts:

> "What I think the DNA material has done is that it has shown, by the almost unbelievable complexity of the arrangements which are needed to produce life, that intelligence must have been involved in getting these extraordinarily diverse elements to work together." When asked how his atheist friends responded, he said: "I have been denounced by my fellow unbelievers for stupidity, betrayal, senility, and everything you could think of, and none of them have read a word that I have ever written."[17]

It seems that one of the reasons that Flew changed his mind is because he saw how easy it is to let preconceived theories and beliefs shape the way we view evidence instead of letting the evidence shape our theories and beliefs. As Flew began to let the truth of the evidence shape his actual beliefs, he changed his mind about God.

In the end, Antony Flew's mind was changed because of the principled practice he followed all of his life: follow the truth wherever it leads. It seems quite logical that if we do not have a great love of truth, we most certainly will never find it.

C.S. LEWIS is among the most influential writers of the twentieth century. Many people are somewhat surprised to learn that Lewis, who was dutifully raised in a traditional Christian household in Ireland, actually became an avowed atheist in his early teens while attending public school at the prestigious Malvern College in England. It would be years later, after World War I, and well into his years at Oxford University, before he began his great search for a deeper and richer understanding of God's existence.

Lewis writes that there were two events in his life that ultimately led him to the Christian faith. The first step began when he read G.K. Chesterton's book *The Everlasting Man*, and the second, he has written, had a "shattering impact" on him. This event occurred one night, when one of the more militant atheists on the Oxford faculty staff, a man by the name of T.D. Weldon, came to his room and confided that he believed the historical authenticity of the Gospels appeared to be surprisingly sound.

This conversation deeply disturbed Lewis. He reasoned that if such a staunch atheist as Weldon thinks the Gospels may be historically true, where does that leave him? Lewis, you see, had always believed the New Testament stories to be nothing more than mere myths; there wasn't a shred of history or practical truth in them.

He began to reason that if the Gospel stories are, in fact, true, then this would mean all other truth would have to fade into insignificance. For the first time, he says, he began to wonder if his whole life was headed in the wrong direction.

Weldon's remarks about the historical authenticity of the Gospels wouldn't let him rest, as the conversation echoed in his memory and continued to haunt him. So, Lewis, a determined seeker of truth, began an investigation.

One of the things we learn about C.S. Lewis is that he was very open-minded and was not afraid of the truth, even if it led him away from his atheistic beliefs with which he had grown so comfortable.

As a professor of English literature at Oxford, he had spent his entire professional life studying ancient manuscripts. And though, up to that time, he had never seriously read the Bible, he nonetheless considered it to be one of the world's great myths, like Norse mythology. The Gospels, Lewis noted, didn't contain the rich, imaginative writing techniques of most ancient writings. With a literary critic's ear for language and meter, Lewis recognized that the New Testament didn't contain the stylized and carefully groomed qualities one would expect in any myth-making culture.

Lewis writes:

> "[The Gospels] appeared to be simple, eye-witness accounts of historical events primarily by Jews who were clearly unfamiliar with the great myths of the pagan world around them…I was by now too experienced in literary criticism to regard the Gospels as myth. They had not the mythological taste."[18]

Lewis continues, emphasizing that the Gospels were different from anything else he had ever read in ancient literature.

> "Now, as a literary historian, I am perfectly convinced, that whatever else the Gospels are, they are not legends. I have read a great deal of legends and am quite clear that they are not the same sort of thing. They are not artistic enough to be

> legends. From an imaginative point of view, they are clumsy; they don't work. Most of the life of Jesus is totally unknown to us and no people building up a legend would allow that to be so."[19]

And so, as an expert in ancient documents and languages, he began to wonder: If these aren't myths and legends, then what are they? Were they truly eyewitness accounts of historical events that actually took place?

Here we have this brilliant man, C.S. Lewis, an expert in ancient literature, a man of integrity and great education, who for so many years had dismissed the Gospels— the most influential body of writing in the Western world—simply because they sounded so unconvincing and without merit.

Everything changed, however, when Weldon, his trusted friend and colleague, an atheist with absolutely no trace of bias or hidden agendas, admitted that he found it highly likely that the Gospels truly did present historically accurate accounts of the life of this man Jesus. This is what caused Lewis to embark on a search for spiritual truth.

So, my challenge to you, the reader, is to follow the truth wherever it leads, always remembering that the truth is your friend. It enables you to believe responsibly. It leads to your ultimate well-being.

2.

The Presence of Evil

"It is considered awkward to use seriously such words as 'good' and 'evil'. . . But if we are to be deprived of [these] concepts, what will be left? We will decline to the status of animals."

—ALEKSANDR SOLZHENITSYN

2.1

Seeking To Understand Evil

ONE OF my favorite authors and apologists, who often speaks to college audiences, recently said:

> "I have never defended the existence of God at a university campus without being asked about this question of evil in the world." [1]

It is clearly the number one issue people contend with when it comes to the existence of God, particularly the God of the Bible who is described as a God of love.

A few years ago, CNN published an article titled "Why I Raise My Children Without God." Instantly it went viral. The author, a young mother named Deborah Mitchell, listed several reasons why she shielded her children from learning about God—most of them variations on the problem of evil. Mitchell argued that a loving God would not allow "murders, child abuse, wars, brutal beatings, torture and millions of heinous acts to be committed throughout the history of mankind."

Having rejected the Christian answer, what did Mitchell offer as an alternative? She proposed a materialistic worldview in which humans are completely determined, without free will.

"We are just a very, very small part of a big, big machine," she intoned, "and the influence we have is miniscule." We must accept "the realization of our insignificance."[2]

I think before proceeding we need to consider the issue of evil. In the above example, how does Ms. Mitchell explain to her children the horrendous deeds that seem to show up daily on the news, whether it be murder, torture, or rape? Has she removed the word "evil" from their vocabulary?

But, what do we mean when we use the word evil? Why are those things evil to begin with? You have to know what evil is before you can discuss it and point to examples of it.

I think that Greg Koukl has provided great insight into this when he says, "…we use the word evil when we see things that are not the way they are supposed to be." It is as if we have some standard of good that we expect people to live by, and evil is at the very bottom of the goodness scale.[3]

However, you have to explain where the goodness scale comes from that enables us to identify evil. Where is the standard of good that makes this notion of evil to be intelligible? Atheists are forced to acknowledge that this is a thorny problem, because who determines the ultimate "good" in life?

Charles Darwin really struggled with this as he considered the descent of man and the origin of evil passions. He concluded that what we today call evil is merely inherited animal passions. The genes of the violent animals I descended from made me do it; I have no free choice in this matter.[4]

This is how Adolf Hitler justified his enormous cruelty by reasoning, "Why should I not be crueler than nature itself?" He saw that nature was naturally cruel and that there was no reason for him not to unleash this cruelty onto the world.

I think sometimes people are shocked that any person might have this type of worldview, but we really should not be surprised. The teaching of evolution is clear that "natural selection depends on death, destruction, and violence of the strong against the weak." This is perfectly natural.[5]

I was reading some interesting words on evil from the well-known historian Andrew Delbanco, who teaches at Columbia University. He says that "a gulf has opened up in our culture between the visibility of evil and the intellectual resources available for coping with it." He argues that modern people attribute all cruelty to psychological reasons, and in the process trivialize the presence of evil in our land. He then tells the story of President Franklin Roosevelt during the Second World War. President Roosevelt, and many of America's intellectual elites, scoffed at the reports they were hearing about the possible acts of genocide toward the Jewish people, and therefore gave no priority to the rescue of these victims. However, late in the war, after the evidence of the Holocaust became more certain, the President was given a book written by the Christian philosopher Søren Kierkegaard. After reading it, he finally had "an understanding of what it is in man that makes it possible...to be so evil." Delbanco, who considers himself a secular liberal, acknowledged that he and his colleagues had lost any concept of evil.[6]

So how does a person with an atheistic worldview deal with the problem of evil and wickedness? He does not have a good basis to be outraged over the evil he sees in the world. Think about it, if in this world you see what you know to be evil and cruel, you have to assume the reality of some type of transcendent standard in order to make your judgment.

The highly respected philosopher Alvin Plantinga had these profound words to say on this issue:

> "Could there really be any such thing as horrifying wickedness [if there were no God and we just evolved]? I don't see how. There can be such a thing only if there is a way that rational creatures are supposed to live, obliged to live... A [secular] way of looking at the world has no place for genuine moral obligation of any sort... and thus no way to say there is such a thing as genuine and appalling wickedness. Accordingly, if you think there really is such a thing as horrifying wickedness (...and not just an illusion of some sort), then you have a powerful...argument [for the reality of God]?"[7]

Plantinga's words are quite powerful. Modern people so easily dismiss God because of the presence of evil in the world. Without realizing it, the notion of evil implies that there is a standard of goodness that has been violated. Who then decides this standard of goodness? (I will take this up in the next essay.)

I believe Tim Keller summed up the words in this essay with this simple explanation:

> "In short, the problem of tragedy, suffering, and injustice is a problem for everyone. It is at least as big a problem for nonbelief in God as for belief. It is therefore a mistake, though an understandable one, to think that if you abandon belief in God it somehow makes the problem of evil easier to handle."[8]

2.2

Who Determines What Is Evil?

WHEN I was a young boy, I remember seeing a movie on television about a true event that was the first big crime of the century (similar to the O.J. Simpson case). It was called the Leopold–Loeb case, and took place in the 1920s.

It involved two teenage boys, 18-year-old Richard Loeb, and his best friend, 17-year-old Nathan Leopold. Loeb was a smart young man and was fascinated with crimes and mysteries. His great desire was to commit the perfect crime. Leopold was equally intelligent and was headed to Harvard Law School, even though he was only 17. Leopard was fascinated with philosophy, particularly the philosophy of Friedrich Nietzsche, and he believed that legal obligations didn't apply to superior beings. And so, when Loeb discussed with him the possibility of trying to commit the perfect crime, he went along with it. They kidnapped a young boy in their neighborhood, and they bludgeoned him to death in the back of their car. They took him to a site and they poured acid all over him, so he wouldn't be recognizable, and dumped him. They eventually were caught, and finally confessed.

Their families were very wealthy and hired the top legal team in the country, headed by Clarence Darrow. Mr. Darrow employed a brilliant legal strategy that saved them from the death sentence. His main argument to the jury (right out of the transcript of the trial):

> "Is there any blame attached because somebody took Nietzsche's philosophy seriously and fashioned his life on it? Your honor, it's hardly fair to hang a 19-year-old boy for the philosophy that was taught him at the University."[9]

In other words, he was saying that you can't execute these young men for following the teaching they received in college. They had followed Nietzsche's godless worldview, and it had become the foundation of their thinking. Darrow's argument prevailed, and they were not executed.

Another way to consider this is to think of Adolf Hitler, whose life was profoundly impacted by Nietzsche's writings. If you were given the opportunity to challenge Hitler face to face and confront him with the great evil of slaughtering millions of innocent people, he would have responded that there is nothing wrong with these actions, and that they are for the common good of the human race. This strikes at the heart of the nature of morality.

Hitler would appeal to the logic of his worldview. He believed that the survival of the fittest is a fact of nature, and he was being consistent with that fact. He clearly believed he was improving the human race by ridding society of inferior beings (the Jews) and creating a master race. He believed there was nothing immoral in what he was doing. If you are an atheist, how do you respond to this logic?

It is important to know that this is not just hypothetical reasoning on my part; this is what Hitler actually believed. On October 10, 1941, Hitler stated:

> "Today war is nothing but a struggle for the riches of nature. By virtue of an inherent law, these riches belong to him who conquers them… That's in accordance with the laws of nature. By means of the struggle, the elites are continually renewed. The law of selection justifies this incessant struggle, by allowing the survival of the fittest. Christianity is a rebellion against natural law, a protest against nature. Taken to

> its logical extreme, Christianity would mean the systematic cultivation of the human failure."[10]

In order to influence the German people's worldview, Hitler ordered that a propaganda film be produced and shown in German movie theaters. In the film, there is a psychiatric institution with a narrator who declares:

> "Wherever fate puts us, whatever station we must occupy, only the strong will prevail in the end. Everything in the natural world that is weak for life will ineluctably be destroyed. In the last few decades, mankind has sinned terribly against the law of natural selection. We haven't just maintained life unworthy of life; we have even allowed it to multiply! The descendants of these sick people look like this!"[11]

It was not surprising that three years later, after the film had been released, the German mental institutions began gassing to death thousands of innocent patients.

It is quite clear that, apart from a transcendent lawgiver, there is no real basis for moral law other than the law of the jungle. As the celebrated atheist Richard Dawkins has put it:

> "This is one of the hardest lessons for humans to learn. We cannot admit that things might be neither good nor evil, neither cruel nor kind, but simply callous—indifferent to all suffering, lacking all purpose."

What is most interesting is, after Germany lost the war, the German Nazi leaders were put on trial at Nuremberg. As the Nuremberg trials began, questions arose over what laws should be used to judge the Nazis. Before the trial began, the Allies had prepared a Charter Tribunal consisting of the rules of procedure, the rules of evidence, and the laws under which the Nazis would be prosecuted. The Nazi defendants claimed that they were being tried by ex post facto laws, and several authorities in international law criticized the Allied judges for the same reasons. The Nazis on trial logically appealed to the fact that they consistently followed the mandates of their country and government and that their actions were in obedience to the laws in effect at the time. They argued that they could not be convicted simply because their behavior deviated from the contrary value system of their conquerors.

The chief prosecutor for the United States at the Nuremberg trials, Robert H. Jackson, appealed to permanent, transcultural values. He appealed to a law beyond the law, a universal law. He said that a system of ethics must point beyond itself—it has to be transcendental, and its basis cannot rest within the finite world. Otherwise, how could one, in good faith, say that the Nazis were wrong in their actions?[12]

2.3

What Is a Human Being?

HARVARD PSYCHOLOGIST B. F. Skinner viewed man as a machine that responds mechanically to stimuli, and he openly mocked the religious view that elevated the dignity of man. He said that he was glad to see the riddance of the sacredness of man, and that his abolition has been long overdue. In his book *Beyond Freedom and Dignity*, Skinner argues that there is no reason to regard human beings as anything other than a product of nature.[13]

But is man really a machine? I am reminded of a significant chess match several years ago, when the computer "Deep Blue" beat the world champion Garry Kasparov. This, of course, caused many pundits to compare machines and humans and, in the process, highlight the similarities. In the eyes of many, we are nothing but sophisticated machines.

Yale professor of computer science David Gelernter strongly disagrees. In an article in *Time Magazine* he says:

> "The idea that Deep Blue has a mind is absurd. How can an object that wants nothing, fears nothing, enjoys nothing, needs nothing and cares about nothing have a mind? It can win at chess, but not because it wants to. It isn't happy when it wins or sad when it loses. What are its apres-match plans if it beats

> Kasparov? Is it hoping to take Deep Pink out for a night on the town?"

He continues:

> "The gap between human and surrogate is permanent and will never be closed. Machines will continue to make life easier, healthier, richer and more puzzling. And humans will continue to care, ultimately, about the same things they always have: about themselves, about one another and, many of them, about God."[14]

Think of the uniqueness of a human being. We have a conscience with the ability to feel, to love, and to experience joy. We have a desire for security and have this unique yearning that our lives matter and are significant. We have the ability to be fearful but also feel peace. There is no other creature in this world that has the uniqueness of a person.

What most people don't seem to realize is how the atheist view of humanity is so diametrically opposed to the Christian view. If there is no God, what is a person? How valuable is human life?

Ingrid Newkirk, co-founder of People for the Ethical Treatment of Animals, says:

> "There is no rational reason for saying that a human being has special rights. A rat is a pig is a dog is a boy."[15]

There are a number of ethicists who argue now that an animal's rights should take precedence over a human's.

A good understanding of the atheistic view of human life can be found in the perspective offered by Dr. Rodney Brooks, who received his PhD in computer science from Stanford. He is a roboticist. He taught robotics for a number of years at MIT, where he was the director of the MIT Computer Science and Artificial Intelligence Laboratory. Brooks says:

> "A human being is nothing but a machine or a big bag of skin full of biomolecules interacting by the laws of physics and chemistry."[16]

This view of man started with Charles Darwin. Many people are not aware of the complete title of his highly influential book, *The Origin of Species by Means of Natural Selection or the Preservation of Favoured Races in the Struggle for Life.* A key idea in the book is how good it is for the least favored races to become extinct. He said:

> "According to the laws of natural selection, the European race will emerge as the distinct species homo sapiens, and all the transitional forms—the gorilla, the chimpanzee, the Negro, and the Australian Aborigine—will be extinguished in the struggle."[17]

Where is this taking us, a world in which human life is nothing more than a product of nature, and that stronger and more favored races will survive, and the weak and disadvantaged will eventually become extinct?

John Lennox has spoken often with Russian intellectuals. Many of them of high standing would remark to him that they truly believed that they could get rid of God and retain a value for human beings. They all acknowledged they were wrong. They said, "We destroyed both God and man."

Viktor Frankl spent several years in a Nazi death camp but never blamed God for the Holocaust. He blamed all of the horror on people who truly lived out their atheistic worldviews. In his book *The Doctor and the Soul,* Frankl says:

> "If we present a man with a concept of man which is not true, we may well corrupt him. When we present man as an automaton of reflexes, as a mind-machine, as a bundle of instincts, as a pawn of drives and reactions, as a mere product of instinct, heredity and environment, we feed the nihilism to which modern man is, in any case, prone."

Frankl went on to say:

> "I became acquainted with the last stage of that corruption in my second concentration camp, Auschwitz. The gas chambers of Auschwitz were the ultimate consequence of the theory that man is nothing but the product of heredity and environment; or as the Nazi liked to say, 'of Blood and Soil.' I am absolutely convinced that the gas chambers of Auschwitz, Treblinka, and Maidanek were ultimately prepared not in some Ministry or other in Berlin, but rather at the desks and lecture halls of nihilistic scientists and philosophers."[18]

These are very sobering words and help us better understand the godless regimes that have no regard for human life.

The famous historian H.G. Wells believed that those in power must take control of the evolutionary process. He was encouraged to see that Lenin's revolution in Russia represented an important step in that direction. He met with Lenin in 1920 and liked the direction Lenin was taking Russia, though he became aware that this new Soviet Union was killing large numbers of people. However, he justified it in his own mind since this was the price that needed to be paid for creating a new humanity. He went along with Lenin that to secure a new future, you had to eliminate the undesirables.[19]

Over time, however, Wells saw the failure of Communism and the devastation it wreaked on the Russian people. Just a year before he died in 1946, he published his final book, *Mind at the End of Its Tether.* As he looked back at the progress of man, he concluded, "There is no way out or round or through the impasse. It is the end."[20]

One of the twentieth century's great poets was W.H. Auden. To escape the war in Europe during the late 1930s, he came to the United States and lived in the Yorkville district of Manhattan. This area was the German-speaking area of the city. World War II had just broken out in 1939, and he went to a local movie theater to watch a documentary showing the Nazi account of their conquest of Poland. Most of the people in the theater were Germans, and when the Polish people appeared on the screen, he was startled to hear the people in the audience shout "Kill them! Kill them!"

Auden was stunned to see this reaction. He realized for the first time, in a flash, that human nature was not good. And it strongly impacted his atheistic worldview. He realized for the first time that he had been seeking to undermine faith in God's absolutes. He saw, and heard, the evil in the chants to kill the Poles. Spurred on by the contradiction in his life, his entire worldview began a transformation that led him to Christianity.[21]

I end this essay with a true story of a woman who came to understand the contradiction in having an atheistic worldview, but then also believing in the value of human beings and human rights. Carolyn Fluehr-Lobban used to teach cultural anthropology, and she believed that all morality is basically socially constructed. Thus, she believed we should never impose our morality on another culture. She was working in Africa and saw the terrible oppression of women. In *The Chronicle of Higher Education,* she wrote a fascinating article about the agony she felt when she tried to tell the leaders of the African societies that what they were doing to women was wrong. They responded, "Don't impose your values on us." They added, "You're imposing your religious beliefs on us."

She retorted that she was not religious. But she began to realize that, of course, she is. She is a secular humanist and believed in human rights. Human rights are not self-evident to everybody. Human rights are not things we can prove. It takes religious commitment. It's a faith assumption.[22]

When you consider the value of human life and evil, which of the two worldviews we have been considering presents a view of life that is in harmony with reality? Can human beings have value and dignity if we are not special creatures, whose lives have been handed down from a higher source? For this reason, God values His people, which gives us our worth and dignity.

2.4

The Value of Human Life

I READ a thought-provoking quote from a secular intellectual. He asked this question:

> "The request to 'feed the hungry' seems to have the most compelling claim on us, but how rational is it?"

Science does not tell us to feed the hungry. Moreover, feeding the hungry is defeating the purpose of natural selection. On the one hand, science seems to suggest against it.

You know, he is right. Human life, if there is no god, is cheap. In a godless universe, man is nothing more than a mass of chemicals.

Friedrich Nietzsche said that humans are merely animals. B. F. Skinner, the famous psychologist at Harvard University, reduced people to the status of a machine. Jean-Paul Sartre, the French existentialist, regarded mankind as nothing more than a "useless passion."

Before he became a Christian and recanted his 'atheistic beliefs', Mortimer Adler, one of the most prominent philosophers of the last century, saw human beings as nothing more than sophisticated animals. For this reason, he said, "There is no logical reason to treat mankind differently from any other animal. Therefore, to exploit minorities or to exterminate the homeless could not be condemned any more than killing steers in a slaughterhouse."[23]

Again, if there is no God, Adler is logically correct.

Contrast this with the life of Mother Teresa, the benevolent Catholic nun who dedicated her life's work to caring for the sick and poor of Calcutta, India. These people lived out their lives in pain, fear, and loneliness. Many times, Mother Teresa was asked why she cared for those who were doomed. She responded along the lines of, "They are created by God; they deserve to die with dignity." She clearly believed that every person is precious and has a great value that was formulated by God's creative act.

So, whose perspective is correct? Over twenty years ago, I was in Germany and had the opportunity to visit Dachau, a Nazi death camp from World War II. It was a sobering experience.

I then read an article in *Christianity Today* that its editor, Philip Yancey, had written. The article summarized an interview that he conducted with a pastor who had fought in World War II and, in fact, had been at Dachau as it was liberated in April 1945. The following is the account of Yancey's experience:

> "It was a blustery Chicago day, and I sat hunched in a wool sweater next to a hissing radiator…The pastor looked off to his right, seeming to focus on a blank space on the wall. He was silent for at least a minute. His eyes moved back and forth rapidly, as if straining to fill in the scene from forty years before. Finally, he spoke, and for the next twenty minutes he recalled the sights, the sounds, and the smells—especially the smells—that greeted his units as they marched through the gates of Dachau.
>
> For weeks, the soldiers had heard wild rumors about the camps, but believing them to be war propaganda, they gave little credence to such rumors. Nothing prepared them, and nothing could have possibly prepared them, for what they found inside.
>
> *'A buddy and I were assigned to one boxcar. Inside were human*

corpses, stacked in neat rows, exactly like firewood. The Germans, ever meticulous, had planned out the rows—alternating the head and feet, accommodating different sizes and shapes of bodies.

Our job was like moving furniture. We would pick up each body— so light!—and carry it to a designated area. Some fellows couldn't do this part. They stood by the barbed wire fences, retching.

I couldn't believe it the first time we came across a person in the pile still alive. But it was true. Incredibly, some of the corpses weren't corpses. They were human beings. We yelled for doctors, and they went to work on these survivors right away.

I spent two hours in that boxcar, two hours that, for me, included every known emotion: rage, pity, shame, revulsion—every negative emotion, I should say. They came in waves, all but the rage. It stayed, fueling our work. We had no other emotional vocabulary for such a scene.

After we had taken the few survivors to a makeshift clinic, we turned our attention to the SS officers in charge of Dachau, who were being held under guard in a bunkhouse. Army Intelligence had set up an interrogation center nearby. It was outside the camp, and to reach it, you had to walk down a ravine through some trees. The captain asked for a volunteer to escort a group of twelve SS prisoners to the interrogation center, and Chuck's hand went straight up.

Chuck was the loudest, most brash, most volatile soldier in our unit. He stood about five-feet four inches tall, but he had overly long arms so that his hands hung down around his knees like a gorilla's. He came from Cicero, a suburb of Chicago, known mainly for its racism and its association with Al Capone. Chuck claimed to have worked for Capone before the war, and not one of us doubted it.

Well, Chuck grabbed a submachine gun and prodded the group of SS prisoners down the trail. They walked ahead of him with their hands locked back behind their heads, their elbows sticking out on either side. A few minutes after they disappeared into the trees, we heard the rattling burp of machine gun in three long bursts of fire. We all ducked; it could have been a German sniper in the woods. But soon Chuck came strolling out, smoke still curling from the tip of his weapon. "They all tried to run away," he said, with a kind of leer.'

I asked if anyone reported what he did or took disciplinary action. The pastor laughed, and then he gave me a 'get-serious-this-is-war' look.

'No, and that's what got to me. It was on that day that I felt called by God to become a pastor. First, there was the horror of the corpses in the boxcar. I could not absorb such a scene. I did not even know such Absolute Evil existed. But when I saw it, I knew beyond doubt that I must spend my life serving whatever opposed such Evil—serving God.

Then came the Chuck incident. I had a nauseating fear that the captain might call on me to escort the next group of SS guards, and even more, dreadful fear that if he did, I might do the same as Chuck. The beast that was within those guards was also with me.'

I could not coax more reminiscing from the pastor that day. Either he had probed the past enough or he felt obligated to move on to our own agenda. But before we left the subject entirely, I asked a question that, as I look back now, seems almost impudent.

'Tell me,' I asked, 'after such a cosmic kind of call to the ministry—confronting the great Evil of the century—how must it feel to fulfill that call by sitting in this office listening to middle-class yuppies like me ramble on about our problems?'

His answer came back quickly, as if he had asked himself that question many times.

'I do see the connection,' he said. 'Without being melodramatic, I sometimes wonder what might have happened if a skilled, sensitive person had befriended the young, impressionable Adolf Hitler as he wandered the streets of Vienna in his confused state. The world might have been spared all that bloodshed at Dachau. I never know who might be sitting in that chair you're occupying right now.

And even if I end up spending my life with "nobodies," I learned in the boxcar that there is no such thing. Those corpses with a pulse were as close to nobodies as you can get: mere skeletons wrapped in papery skin. But I would have done anything to keep those poor, ragged souls alive. Our medics stayed up all night to save them; some in our company lost their lives to liberate them. There are no "nobodies." I learned that day in Dachau what "the image of God" in a human being is all about.'[24]

Ask yourself a very simple question. Do you believe that you—and all other human beings—are unique in a way that cannot be explained by the idea that you are a sophisticated animal or an elaborate machine? Do your family members and all the people in your life have value beyond the emotional, physical, and financial support that you get from them? The only way that human life can be extolled and held sacred is if God in His divine wisdom created humanity as a reflection of Himself.

2.5

Why All the Violence?

STEPHEN PADDOCK was an American mass murderer responsible for the 2017 Las Vegas shooting in which he opened fire into a crowd of 22,000 who were attending a country music festival. It was the deadliest mass shooting by a lone shooter in United States history. There were 58 fatalities and a number of wounded people as well. Afterwards, Paddock took his own life.

I remember how difficult it was for people to wrap their heads around this horrific event. The brutality and senselessness of it left most people bewildered, confused, and angry. The reason is clearly because we all recognize the great value of human life.

NPR's Steve Inskeep interviewed Darrell Gibbs, the father of a wounded shooting victim, in a Las Vegas hotel. He and relatives were taking shifts by his daughter's hospital bed. Gibbs works as a federal corrections counselor, meaning he advises inmates as they leave a Texas prison.

Inskeep questions Gibbs on how he first heard the news, his daughter's injuries and expected recovery, and, finally, why this has happened.

Inskeep: *"You don't blame the gun for this."*
Gibbs: *"Absolutely not."*
Inskeep: *"You blame the person."*

Gibbs: *"Of course."*
Inskeep: *"What do you think is causing these mass shootings?"*
Gibbs: *"A godless society."*[25]

Though I am sure there were those who sneered at this response, I believe it is a valid observation. If there is no God, then what is a human being? Are we more than a mass of chemicals that are here by chance? The famous Harvard psychologist B.F. Skinner, who was an atheist, said there is no reason to regard human beings as anything other than a product of nature. He believed there was no logical reason to treat mankind differently from any other animal. Think about how easily we slaughter thousands of cattle each day in a slaughterhouse. This seems to be how Stephen Paddock regarded all of the people he shot at random.

I am reminded of the words of Jeffrey Dahmer, arguably one of the most evil serial killers ever to live, not only because he killed so many innocent victims but also because he cannibalized those he had murdered. Shortly before his death, he gave an interview from prison that was aired on ABC News. This is what he said:

> "When I was in high school, I found within myself the desire to torture animals. I did not believe in God, I did not believe we were here for a purpose...Given that I was not here for a purpose and I am going to die and that is the end of me, I could not find sufficient reason to deny the satisfactions of my desires."

Then, he tells us that as he got older, he eventually reached the point where torturing animals no longer satisfied him, saying, "At that point, I decided I'll torture human beings." Based on his view of life and morality, he plainly admitted, "I could not think of a reason why I shouldn't, given my view of reality."[26]

Now, I'm not suggesting atheists end up being serial killers, but it is obvious there was a real disconnect in Dahmer's life, which stemmed from his godless worldview. He admits it.

Probably the most famous and well-known atheist ever to live was the German philosopher Friedrich Nietzsche. He challenged his atheist friends that if they were going to give up belief in the Christian God, they would also have to give up Christian morality, particularly pity, compassion, and the value of human beings.

Nietzsche no doubt would tell any atheist who felt for those who were shot in Las Vegas to quit being such wimps and whiners, and that they should expect violence and suffering in the world. It is the law of nature, which is naturally violent.

I close this essay with a very sobering satirical poem by English journalist Steve Turner. Many people call it the "Atheist Creed."

A creed, of course, is a fundamental belief, a kind of guiding principle. Turner calls this piece "Creed," and it attempts to reveal how modern people think and what they believe.

We believe in Marxfreudanddarwin.
We believe everything is OK
as long as you don't hurt anyone
to the best of your definition of hurt,
and to the best of your knowledge.

We believe in sex before, during, and after marriage.
We believe in the therapy of sin.
We believe that adultery is fun.

We believe that sodomy is OK.
We believe that taboos are taboo.
We believe that everything's getting better
despite evidence to the contrary.

The evidence must be investigated
and you can prove anything with evidence.
We believe there's something in horoscopes,
UFO's and bent spoons.

Jesus was a good man just like Buddha,
Mohammed, and ourselves.
He was a good moral teacher though we think
His good morals were bad.

We believe that all religions are basically the same—
at least the one that we read was.
They all believe in love and goodness.
They only differ on matters of
creation, sin, heaven, hell, God, and salvation.

We believe that after death comes the Nothing
Because when you ask the dead what happens they say nothing.
If death is not the end, if the dead have lied,
then it's compulsory heaven for all
excepting perhaps Hitler, Stalin, and Genghis Khan.

We believe in Masters and Johnson.
What's selected is average.
What's average is normal.
What's normal is good.

We believe in total disarmament.
We believe there are direct links between
warfare and bloodshed.
Americans should beat their guns into tractors.
And the Russians would be sure to follow.

We believe that man is essentially good.
It's only his behavior that lets him down.
This is the fault of society.
Society is the fault of conditions.
Conditions are the fault of society.

We believe that each man must find the truth that is right for him.
Reality will adapt accordingly.

> The universe will readjust. History will alter.
>
> We believe that there is no absolute truth
> excepting the truth that there is no absolute truth.
> We believe in the rejection of creeds,
> And the flowering of individual thought.
>
> If chance be the Father of all flesh,
> disaster is his rainbow in the sky,
> and when you hear
>
> State of Emergency!
> Sniper Kills Ten!
> Troops on Rampage!
> Whites go Looting!
> Bomb Blasts School!
>
> It is but the sound of man worshipping his maker.[27]

Turner is pointing out the incoherence of modern belief and its ramifications. He is saying that we should expect violence and evil because of today's worldview that is shaping people's lives.

This seems to be where we are headed as a nation. I am reminded how God, in the Old Testament, lays out the choice we have to make as we seek to live our lives and build our communities:

> "I call heaven and earth to witness against you today, that I have set before you life and death, the blessing and the curse. So choose life in order that you may live, you and your descendants, by loving the Lord your God, by obeying His voice, and by holding fast to Him; **for this is your life.**" (Deuteronomy 30:19,20)

This is the very means by which God addresses the problem of evil.

2.6

Hope for a Broken World

A NUMBER of years ago I heard a prominent lecturer and author, Ron Carlson, speak on the value of human life. He spoke of visiting the Cambodian border back in the 1970s when more than 300,000 refugees were looking for a place to settle. They had escaped the Cambodian massacre but had nowhere to go.

Carlson was stunned that all these Buddhist refugees were coming from Cambodia and Laos, yet there were no Buddhists lending a hand or taking care of them. Nor were there any Hindus or Muslims. The only people taking care of all these refugees were Christians from Christian mission and relief organizations.

Carlson approached a man who had lived in this area for twenty years and asked him,

> "Why, in a Buddhist country, with Buddhist refugees, are there no Buddhists here caring for their brothers?"

The reason he received:

> "Ron, have you ever seen what Buddhism does to a nation or a people? Buddha taught that each man is an island unto himself. Buddha said, 'If someone is suffering, that is his karma.' You are not to interfere with another person's karma because he is purging himself through suffering and reincar-

nation! Buddha said, 'You are to be an island unto yourself.'"

This leader of the relief effort continued,

> "Ron, the only people that have a reason to be here today taking care of these 300,000 refugees are Christians. It is only in Christianity that people have a basis for human value; that people are important enough to educate and care for."[28]

The Christian view of life is that people are of such great value because they are created in the image of God.

In his well-documented book *How Christianity Changed the World*, Alvin Schmidt shows how the moral, biblical worldview of Christianity has had such a powerful and positive influence on the world. Through the historical record, he demonstrates the following:

- The idea of human rights came straight from the Bible, as God places a high view of human life and its sanctity.
- Christianity greatly elevated and exalted the value of women. Christ raised the dignity, freedom, and the rights of women to a level previously unknown in all other cultures in history.
- Where did the idea of philanthropy come from? American historian and educator of European history Carlton Hayes said, "From the wellsprings of Christian compassion our Western civilization has drawn its inspiration and its sense of duty for feeding the hungry, giving drink to the thirsty, looking after the homeless, clothing the naked, tending the sick, and visiting the prisoner."
- Biblical teaching was behind establishing hospitals, creating mental institutions, professionalizing medical nursing, and founding The Red Cross.
- Slavery was accepted by virtually every culture in history, as far back as anyone can remember.

It never occurred to anyone that it is wrong. But the abolition of slavery and the rejection of racial segregation go back to the earliest teachings of Christianity. The great historian Will Durant made it clear that Christianity was not a segregated religion.

> *"It offered itself without restriction to all individuals, classes, and nations; it was not limited to one people . . ."*[29]

Matthew Parris is a well-known South African-British journalist and broadcaster who served a number of years in the British Parliament.

Parris spent his childhood in the African country of Malawi and, forty-five years after leaving, returned to help rural African communities install water pumps, giving them access to clean water.

Parris was an atheist. His visit renewed his faith in the development of charities. However, it caused a crisis of faith for him as an atheist. He was shocked at the enormous contribution to the good of Africa as a result of Christian evangelism. It was not at all compatible with his atheistic worldview, and he finally had to admit how transformative Christianity was in his native country. It was unlike any other form of aid or charity being carried out in all of Africa.

Parris acknowledges that this was not in harmony with his atheistic beliefs. It did not fit his ideological beliefs nor his atheistic worldview. It proved to be embarrassing to his belief that God does not exist.[30]

As author Paul Chamberlain described it, Parris found the evangelism of Christians to be distinctly different from the work of secular non-governmental organizations and government endeavors. As good as the work done by these secular organizations is, he declares, it will never be sufficient, nor will education and training. The difference Christianity offers, he says, is a change of people's hearts.

> *"It brings a spiritual transformation. The rebirth is real. The change is good."*[31]

This is what is so unique about Christianity. It is not a religion where you attempt to follow laws and regulations. Christ seeks to work in our hearts and to empower us. Christianity is about the life of God working in the hearts and souls of men and women.

2.7

A Different Perspective on Pain and Suffering

MODERN PEOPLE seem to struggle with the issue of pain and suffering more than anyone else in history. Here in the Western world, we live in such prosperity yet struggle so much more with affliction than people in other parts of the world. Author Philip Yancey says:

> "Books on the problem of pain divide neatly into two groupings. The older ones, by people like Aquinas, Bunyan, Donne, Luther, Calvin, and Augustine, ungrudgingly accept pain and suffering as God's usual agents. These authors do not question God's actions. They merely try to 'justify the ways of God to man.' The authors wrote with confidence, as if the sheer force of their reasoning could calm emotional responses to suffering.
>
> Modern books on pain make a sharp contrast. Their authors assume that the amount of evil and suffering in the world cannot be matched with the traditional view of a good and loving God. God is thus bumped from a 'friend of the court' position to the box reserved for the defendant. 'How can you possible justify yourself, God?' these angry moderns seem to say. Many of them adjust their notion of God, either by redefining His love or by questioning His power to control evil.

> When you read the two categories of books side by side, the change in tone is quite striking. It's as if we in modern times think we have a corner on the suffering market. Do we forget that Luther and Calvin lived in a world without ether and penicillin, when life expectancy averaged thirty years, and that Bunyan and Donne wrote their greatest works, respectively, in a jail and a plague quarantine room? Ironically, the modern authors—who live in princely comfort, toil in climate-controlled offices, and hoard elixirs in their medicine cabinets—are the ones smoldering with rage."[32]

Author Tim Keller encounters many religious skeptics in Manhattan where he works, and so many of them are skeptics because of the pain and suffering they see in life. How could a good God, a just God, a loving God allow such misery, pain, and anguish to exist?

However, Keller points out on the flip side that he has seen many people find God and transformation in the midst of pain and suffering. Adversity moves them toward God instead of away from Him. He says troubled times awakens people out of the belief that they are sufficient without God. This often leads people into a serious search of the divine.[33]

C.S. Lewis seemed to have a good grasp on this. In his book *The Problem of Pain,* he says:

> "Pain insists upon being attended to. God whispers to us in our pleasure...but shouts in our pain; it is His megaphone to rouse a deaf world."

He goes on to say:

> "No doubt pain as God's megaphone is a terrible instrument; it may lead to final unrepented rebellion. But it gives the only opportunity the bad man can have for amendment. It removes the veil; it plants the flag of truth within the fortress of a rebel soul."[34]

Dinesh D'Souza speaks of Bart Ehrman, an author, scripture scholar, and former Christian who abandoned his faith because of unspeakable suffering he saw out in the world. He said, "I could no longer reconcile the claims of faith with the facts of life." What is interesting is that Ehrman acknowledges that he personally has never experienced any real suffering in his own life. What troubles him most is the suffering of people in Asia, Africa, and South America. Yet, ironically this is where Christianity is flourishing in the places where the suffering is the greatest.[35]

Historian Philip Jenkins says that in third world countries, suffering turns people toward God. He says,

> "Christianity is flourishing wonderfully among the poor and persecuted, while it atrophies among the rich and secure."[36]

I love the story that Andrea Dilley tells about her life. She was raised by medical missionaries in Kenya and was exposed to a great deal of suffering and death. As a teenager, she began to question her faith and the goodness of God. When she got into her 20s she completely rejected God and Jesus. What drove her away was her anger at God over the suffering and injustice in the world.

She shares how one evening she got into a philosophical discussion with a young man who, like her, did not believe in God, but also did not believe in an absolute moral law. She found herself in a real argument with him, saying, "If morality is subjective, you cannot say Hitler was wrong. You can't condemn evil." It then powerfully struck her that she was arguing with him from a theistic perspective. She said:

> "When people ask me, what drove me out the doors of the church and then what brought me back, my answer to both questions is the same. I left the church in part because I was mad at God about human suffering and injustice. And I came back to church because of that same struggle. I realized that

> I couldn't even talk about justice without standing inside of a theistic framework. In a naturalistic worldview, a parentless orphan in the slums of Nairobi can only be explained in terms of survival of the fittest. We're all just animals slumming it in a godless world, fighting for space and resources. The idea of justice doesn't really mean anything. To talk about justice, you have to talk about objective morality, and to talk about objective morality, you have to talk about God."

She logically concluded that without God and an absolute moral law, justice is a meaningless word.[37]

What I like about Andrea Dilley is her integrity. She rejected a belief in God because of the pain and suffering that she saw out in the world. She did not realize how her new belief in atheism contradicted her everyday life experience. Her belief in the value of human life and justice came very natural to her. She recognized it to be true. She did not see the contradiction in her life until she got into a discussion with a young man who did not live with that same contradiction. He was an atheist and recognized in his worldview, morality is subjective and therefore you cannot say Hitler's actions were evil.

To Dilley's credit, she recognized this massive contradiction and was not willing to live with it. She knew in her heart that human beings are of great value and need to be treated with dignity and respect. So she changed her mind and embraced the Christian worldview because it is consistent with the real world in which she lives.

2.8

Why Does God Allow Evil?

The question that plagues the minds of so many is this: Why does God allow evil to flourish, when He could so easily prevent it? What we need to understand is that evil, pain, and suffering are the results of two principles that God has woven into our earthly existence.

The first principle has to do with the physical world we live in. There are certain natural laws that give order and stability to life. The second principle is human freedom. We have the freedom to make choices and decisions. It is this freedom that makes it possible for us to truly love. This is why we are human beings and not robotic machines as so many atheists believe us to be.

Author Philip Yancey had this to say about these two principles:

> "By committing himself to those two principles, both good principles in themselves, God allowed for the possibility of their abuse. For example, water proves useful to us and all creation because of its "softness," its liquid state, and its specific gravity. Yet those very properties open up its rather disagreeable capacity to drown us—or the even more alarming possibility that we may drown someone else.
>
> Take another example, from wood. It bears the fruit of trees, supports leaves to provide shade, and shelters birds and

> squirrels. Even when taken from the tree, wood is valuable. We use it as fuel to warm ourselves, and as construction material to build houses and furniture. The essential properties of wood—hardness, unpliability, flammability—make possible these useful functions.
>
> But as soon as you plant a tree with those properties in a world peopled by free human beings, you introduce the possibility of abuse. A free man may pick up a chunk of wood and take advantage of its firmness by bashing the head of another man. God could, I suppose, reach down each time and transform the properties of wood into those of sponge, so that the club would bounce off lightly. But that is not what he is about in the world. He has set into motion fixed laws that can be perverted to evil by our misguided freedom."[38]

A question that I often get from people is "Couldn't God have created a world where it is not possible to experience pain, evil, and suffering?" My response is, it is not possible if we are going to be truly human with free wills.

Dr. John Hick, a theologian, wrote a book titled *Philosophy of Religion.* In the book, he tries to envision a utopian world, where we still have free will but there is no pain and suffering. Hick concluded that the consequences would be far-reaching and life would just not work.

> "For example, no one could ever injure anyone else. The murderer's knife would turn into paper or his bullets into thin air. Fraud, deceit, conspiracy, and treason would somehow always leave the fabric of society undamaged. There would never be failure because failure is one of the most painful experiences of life. You would not have to take care of your health, there would be no cancer or heart attacks. You would not have to try hard at relationships because there would be no pain from rejection. There would be no pain from divorce. So, people could live as reckless as they desire and not have to worry about the consequences."

Hick goes on to say:

> "Courage and fortitude would have no point in an environment in which there is, by definition, no danger or difficulty. Generosity, kindness, the agape aspect of love, prudence, unselfishness, and all other ethical notions which presuppose life in an objective environment could not even be formed. Consequently, such a world, however well it might promote pleasure, would be very ill-adapted for the development of moral qualities of human personality. In relation to this purpose it might be the worst of all possible worlds.

It would seem then, that an environment intended to make possible the growth in free beings of the finest characteristics of personal life, must have a good deal in common with our present world. It must operate according to general and dependable laws; and it must involve real dangers, difficulties, problems, obstacles, and possibilities of pain, failure, sorrow, frustration, and defeat."[39]

Hick concludes that this world which has the potential for pain and evil also provides the opportunity for growth, character development, and what Hick calls "soul making."

The second principle involving human freedom is at the heart of being human. God did not create evil; He created the possibility of evil by giving us freedom. Evil is nothing more than the corruption of that which God intended for good. It is logically impossible for Him to create a world in which people have genuine freedom yet without the potential to do that which is depraved or even evil. If God had created us without freedom, we would have a world without humans and a world without love.

God wanted to create a special type of creature that could relate to Him and to others through love, that we might love God, and others, in a meaningful way. True love cannot be forced, it must be freely chosen. However, by giving us this choice, there is also the built-in possibility that we may hate and harm others.

As we look at our world today, it is hard to deny that human depravity has been empirically verified over time. It is also clear that humanity, despite its creative brilliance and the obvious need for great improvement, can't produce a good and perfect society due, in large part, to man's naturally depraved and self-centered nature. As a result, we easily gravitate toward a life of evil and self-destruction.

One of the reasons God sent Jesus into the world is to deliver us from ourselves. So, there is a big question that needs to be answered.

Is it possible for God to change a person's heart? Can He really transform hate to love, selfishness to selflessness, meanness to kindness, and misery into joy?

I remember reading a remarkable book many years ago. In *Through the Valley of the Kwai,* Dr. Ernest Gordon recounts his experience in a Japanese labor prison camp during World War II.

He spoke of how death was in the air and was the chief topic of conversation. He described the inhumane living conditions to which the prisoners were subjected.

> "As conditions steadily worsened, as starvation, exhaustion, and disease took an ever-increasing toll, the atmosphere in which we lived became poisoned by selfishness, hate, and fear. We were slipping rapidly down the slope of degradation.... We lived by the law of the jungle....'I look after myself and to hell with everyone else'....The weak were trampled underfoot, the sick ignored or resented, the dead forgotten. When a man lay dying we had no word of comfort for him. When he cried we averted our heads. Men cursed the Japanese, their neighbours, God....We had no church, no chaplains, no services.... many had turned to religion for the first time. But the crutch had not supported them; so they had thrown it away....We had long since resigned ourselves to being derelicts."

Then several incidents took place that began to transform the prison camp. Several of the prisoners, who were devout Christians, sacrificed their lives for other prisoners. In one situation a man was sick and dying, and his Christian friend would draw his own ration but wouldn't eat it. He would take it to his friend and insist that he eat it instead. Over time, the sick man got better, but his friend finally collapsed and died from starvation.

> "One day Gordon was approached by an Australian sergeant. He said that he and his men wanted to explore Christianity. He said, 'Maybe there is something to it that we haven't understood.' And they knew that Gordon had a Bible.
>
> At their first meeting, there were several dozen men in attendance. Gordon would read and expound on the New Testament. They had discussions about their own inner questioning and their desire for spiritual truth."

Through the Bible readings, they came to know Jesus. They realized He understood them because of what He had faced himself. They began to conclude that Jesus, the carpenter from Nazareth, was the incarnate Word. Gordon said:

> "In the fellowship of freedom and love, we found truth, and with the truth a wonderful sense of unity, of harmony, of peace."

The numbers continued to grow. As more and more men put their faith in Christ, they developed a keener insight into life and its complexities. As Gordon described it:

> "We were learning what it means to be alive—to be human. As we became more aware of our responsibility to God the Father, we realized that we were put in this world not to be served but to serve. This truth touched and influenced many of us, even those who shunned any religious quest. There was a general reawakening. Men began to smile— even to laugh and to sing."

He describes the first Communion, which was quite memorable.

> "With expectant hearts, men had come to receive the strength that only God could give. The elements were of our daily life—rice baked into the form of bread and fermented rice water. The solemn words of the fraction were said.
>
> We broke the bread as it was passed to us and then passed it to our neighbor.
>
> The elements were returned to the Table, a prayer of Thanksgiving said, a hymn sung, and a blessing given. We slipped quietly away into the singing silence of the night, cherishing as we did so our experience of the communion of saints. The Holy Spirit had made us one with our neighbors, one with those at home, one with the faithful in every land, in every age, one with the disciples.
>
> All the while, our own future was unpredictable. We didn't know what the Japanese might have in store for us. We had no assurance that we would ever again see home or those we loved."

Gordon concludes this extraordinary and moving testimony, saying:

> "Whatever happened, we knew that Jesus, our leader, would never fail us. As He had been faithful to His disciples in the first century, He would be faithful to us in the twentieth."[40]

As you read this story, you see the clear presence of evil, as these men were slipping rapidly down the scale of degradation. Though they were all allied soldiers, they were living by the rule of the jungle in order to survive. However, it seems many of them instinctively knew that this was not the way to live. They turned to the only one who might deliver them: Jesus. What Gordon had witnessed in the lives of these prisoners was a spiritual transformation. It was real. It was literally God at work in the hearts of these men. This, I contend, is the only real hope against the evil in our world.

3.

The Moral Argument

"There is truth, and there is falsehood. There is good, and there is evil. There is happiness, and there is misery. There is that which ennobles, and there is that which demeans. There is that which puts you in harmony with yourself, with others, with the universe, and with God, and there is that which alienates you from yourself, and from the world, and from God . . . The greatest error in modern times is the confusion between these orders."

—CHARLES MALIK

3.1
Morality and Atheism

HOW DO we determine what is moral if there is no God who reveals to us what is right or wrong? How do we determine what is moral or immoral? Is it determined by our feelings, by our ability to reason?

If there is no God, who or what is a guiding force in our lives? We must conclude what Richard Dawkins rationally describes:

> "In a universe of blind physical forces and genetic replication, some people are going to get hurt, other people are going to get lucky, and you won't find any rhyme or reason to it, nor any justice. The universe we observe has precisely the properties we should expect if there is at bottom, no design, no purpose, no evil, and no good. Nothing but blind pitiless indifference, DNA neither knows or cares. DNA just is. And we dance to its music."[1]

Think about what he said. If God does not exist, then what are we as human beings? We are purposeless products of biological evolution, which means all morality is subjective. It is based on your opinion.

This has such an impact on a culture when there is no moral compass. You just follow your DNA, wherever it leads you. Richard Dawkins admitted this in a radio interview with radio host Justin Brierley, as Dawkins makes it clear that human morality is nothing more than the outcome of the evolutionary process:

> BRIERLEY: *"When you make a value judgment, don't you immediately step yourself outside of this evolutionary process and say that the reason this is good is that it's good? And you don't have any way to stand on that statement."*
>
> DAWKINS: *"My value judgment itself could come from my evolutionary past."*
>
> BRIERLEY: *"So therefore it's just as random in a sense as any product of evolution."*
>
> DAWKINS: *"You could say that…Nothing about it makes it more probable that there is anything supernatural."*
>
> BRIERLEY: *"Ultimately, your belief that rape is wrong is as arbitrary as the fact that we've evolved five fingers rather than six."*
>
> DAWKINS: *"You could say that, yeah."*[2]

This is astonishing that the world's most prominent atheist could not emphatically say that rape is immoral. Though he may not believe this is true within his heart, he seeks to be a consistent Darwinian atheist.

However, Dawkins does believe that it is not good for a society always to follow Darwinian morality because it is "ruthless." He says,

> "I have always said that I am a passionate anti-Darwinian when it comes to the way we should organize our lives and morality. We want to avoid basing our society on Darwinian principles."[3]

Dawkins, on the one hand, says that we live our lives based on our DNA, but then introduces a moral code by telling us not to follow our DNA. The more I read of Richard Dawkins, the more I recognize how inconsistent he can be.

The individual who has had the most to say about atheism and morality is the great German philosopher Friedrich Nietzsche. He clearly stated that there is no absolute right or wrong. For this reason, he had much contempt for Christianity, because it elevated such beliefs as love, morality, and humility. You can't build a civilization of power on these beliefs.[4]

Nietzsche predicted that the English-speaking world would seek to abandon a belief in God, but would attempt to hold on to Christian values. However, he predicted correctly that when societies reject God, Christian morality itself will eventually disappear. The reason is because it will be more difficult to motivate people to be moral, for they will naturally follow their selfish instincts and desires.[5]

Dr. Arthur Leff, now deceased, was a brilliant professor at Yale Law School. Back in 1979, he published an article in the *Duke Law Journal* titled "Unspeakable Ethics, Unnatural Law." Today, it's considered a very important and prominent essay. It is uncertain what Leff believed about God, but what troubled him was that if there is no God, then there's no way that one can make any kind of case for human morality, particularly human rights. Here is a paraphrased summary of what he said:

You can say it is wrong for a majority to take advantage of any minority by force, but that is an opinion and not an argument. You can assert all sorts of things, but what you cannot do is say one point of view is morally right and all others are not. If someone says it is all right to enslave a minority, and you say no, it is wrong, who is to say your view of morality is right and theirs is wrong? Maybe it helps to frame it this way: if there is no God, who among us gets to impose their will on everyone else? Who gets to establish the moral laws that people are to follow? These questions are so intellectually troubling that you would think there would be more legal and ethical thinkers trying to come to grips with this.[6]

Leff's words suggest that if there is a God, then He would make the law for us to follow. We'd base our law on Him. And this, by the way, is how Western civilization was built, with biblical truth as its foundation. We require a moral foundation on which to build a culture. As T.S. Eliot penned many years ago:

> "It is in Christianity that our arts have developed; it is in Christianity that the laws of Europe… have been rooted."

Returning to Leff's argument, his words also suggest that if there is no God, then moral law has to be grounded in human opinion. So, we must ask, who gets to establish their human opinion as law so that everyone has to obey it? Why should your view of morality have privilege over my view? Ultimately, what you end up with is that those in power will make sure their moral values prevail. Of course, that's what happened in Nazi Germany.

3.2

Christian Morality—Does It Really Matter?

PHILIP YANCEY shared some interesting words about the nature of Christianity and the difference it makes when it is integrated in a person's life. He speaks of certain benefits that are a by-product of the Christian life. He says, "I am a Christian not because Jesus' way benefits society but because I believe it is true. If true, it ***should*** create the conditions in which human life works best."[7]

Modern people don't seem to buy into Yancey's view of life and morality, because they see Christian morality as being restrictive, that it seeks to take away your freedom. However, have you ever thought that Christian morality is more like an owner's manual that fits your design as a human being? If you align your life with the owner's manual, your life will flourish. This is what Yancey seems to be saying.

The highly respected criminologist Byron Johnson, in his book, *More God, Less Crime: Why Faith Matters and How It Could Matter More,* says:

> "Religion is a powerful antidote to crime. It clearly impacts the rates of drug use, violence, and gang activity in the inner city. This is why Eugene Rivers, a pastor in Brooklyn, says, "If you want to help underprivileged youth, we have two options: It's either barbed wire and more black juvenile

> super predators, or civil society and stronger black churches. It's that simple.'"[8]

German philosopher Jürgen Habermas says, "Democracy requires of its citizens qualities that it cannot provide." He recognized that free societies depend on their citizens to act morally and responsibly. Habermas is agnostic, but he stunned his colleagues when he said that Western civilization and its legacy of justice and human rights was the direct heir of the Judeo–Christian values and ethics. He said, "We continue to draw on the substance of this heritage. Everything else is just idle post-modern talk."[9]

I love the story of the well-known social critic Dennis Prager, who was participating in a debate with the atheist philosopher from Oxford, Jonathan Glover. Apparently, Glover was speaking of all the horrors of religion over the years. Prager then asked a most provocative question:

> "If you, Professor Glover, were stranded at the midnight hour in a desolate Los Angeles street and if, as you stepped out of your car with fear and trembling, you were suddenly to hear the weight of pounding footsteps behind you, and you saw ten burly young men who had just stepped out of a dwelling coming toward you, would it or would it not make a difference to you to know that they were coming from a Bible study?"

Glover conceded that it would make a difference.[10]

Think about why it makes a difference. Think about how your worldview impacts the way you regard a human being. If I believe a person has great value as one who is designed in the image of God, I will treat them with dignity and respect. However, if you see life from a godless perspective and human beings are nothing more than a chance product of nature, why not take advantage of them, mug them and steal their wallet.

I think, clearly, Christian virtue and morality make a difference in a person's life and a community whose citizens subscribe to a Christian worldview. Unfortunately, the Christian view of morality seems to be waning in the Western world.

In a very open interview with the *Chicago Sun Times,* the famous atheist philosopher Will Durant declared his belief that common people's lives will fall apart morally if they believe God does not exist. This prediction is what I believe we are seeing come to pass in our land. What is interesting is what Durant says about his own life. He said that he was able to survive morally because he retained the Christian moral code he received during his youth. He acknowledged he had discarded his faith but still retained the morals he had learned growing up. He then made this thoughtful observation:

> "You and I are living on a shadow…because we are operating on the Christian ethical code which was given us, infused with the Christian faith…But what will happen to our children? We are not giving them an ethic warmed up with a religious faith. They are living on the shadow of a shadow."[11]

These words were spoken over forty years ago and his prediction seems to be accurate. It is difficult to live on a shadow, and even more so on a shadow's shadow. However, this is inevitable if you attempt to live without God.

Lord Acton, the great English historian, confirms Durant's observation when he made these remarks about the necessity of having a spiritual foundation.

> "A person's spiritual underpinnings creates an invisible yoke of duty on every citizen. It gives a reason to deny self-interest, to obey the law, to sacrifice for others. However, when we abandon our spiritual roots," he says, "duty loses its hold on our hearts. Crime and lawlessness are then unleashed."[12]

In this essay, I have argued that God has given us moral truth to live by, because He knows what we need in order to live a vibrant healthy life. Another way to see this is to realize that God is like our doctor, who prescribes what we need for our bodies. He does not make up arbitrary suggestions but tells us what to do to stay healthy. The doctor knows and understands the design of the body; if we fail to listen to Him, we risk jeopardizing our health.

We have been given a moral compass to help us address the confusion around us and one that enables us to know the path to go down. This has been found to be objectively true in the research of Guenter Lewy.

An author and political scientist, Lewy has been a faculty member at Columbia University, Smith College, and the University of Massachusetts. Back in the early 1990s, he set out to write a book on why America does not need religion. He saw many of his conservative colleagues taking the position that religion is foundational to morality and social stability, and he intended to prove them wrong. In his own words, he intended "to make a defense of secular humanism and ethical relativism." He wanted to prove that they were "damned wrong."

After extensive research, the sheer weight of the evidence caused Lewy to change his mind. Instead, with academic integrity, he ended up writing his book *Why America Needs Religion,* arguing that religion, particularly Christianity, leads to lower rates of almost every social pathology—including crime, drug abuse, teenage pregnancy, and family breakdown. He clearly recognized the positive influence Christianity makes on people's attitudes and intentions. He saw unmistakably how it instills responsibility, moral integrity, compassion, and generosity. Lewy concluded:

> "Contrary to the expectation of the Enlightenment, freeing individuals from the shackles of traditional religion does not result in their moral uplift. To the contrary, the evidence now shows clearly that no society has yet been successful in teaching morality without religion."[13]

Lewy makes a strong argument that biblical morality makes a difference when it is followed out in the real world. The only way to explain the outcome of his research is to recognize that when people's lives are lined up with the objective structure of God's moral law, they are happier and healthier.

3.3

Can We Be Moral Without God?

IT IS hard to believe, but Richard Dawkins once acknowledged, "It is pretty hard to get objective morality without religion." Since he did not believe in God, it is only natural that he did not believe in objective morality. It could not exist.[14]

However, we clearly have a hard time living without it.

In a key scene from a provocative movie that came out almost twenty-five years ago, "Grand Canyon," featuring Kevin Kline and Danny Glover, the main character, played by Kline, has been to a professional basketball game and veers off the crowded interstate to take a shortcut to get home. Unfortunately, in the process, he soon finds himself in a crime-ridden neighborhood, lost. When he pulls to a stop, the Lexus that he's driving suddenly stalls.

He immediately calls a wrecker service, and while he's waiting, you see these pretty rough teenagers come out of the shadows. They see what they've found, and they're getting ready to ...well, we don't know exactly, because right when they're going to do some serious damage, Danny Glover comes to the rescue. Glover drives up in the wrecker, and, as he steps out to hook up the car, these thugs begin to protest because here they have a guy at their mercy. He drives an expensive car, he's a well-dressed lawyer, and he appears to be someone who could be carrying a great deal of money. Glover takes the leader of the group aside and announces firmly,

> "Man, the world ain't supposed to work like this. Maybe you don't know that, but this ain't the way it's supposed to be. I'm supposed to be able to do my job without asking you if I can. That dude *[referring to Kline]* is supposed to be able to wait with his car without you ripping him off. Everything's supposed to be different than what it is [here]."

Life, the way it's supposed to be. Danny Glover's character was referring to a type of moral behavior that we expect from human beings. There seems to be a right way to live. But who makes that determination?

Donald Miller, in his wonderful book *Blue Like Jazz*, shares this about one of his friends.

> "I know someone who has twice cheated on his wife, whom I don't even know. He told me this over coffee because I was telling him how I thought, perhaps man was broken, how, for man, doing good and moral things was like swimming upstream. He wondered if God had mysteriously told me about his infidelity. He squirmed a bit and then spoke to me as if I were a priest. He confessed everything. I told him I was sorry, that it sounded terrible. And it did sound terrible. His body was convulsed in guilt and self-hatred. He said he would lie down next to his wife at night feeling walls of concrete between their hearts. He had secrets. She tries to love him, but he knows he doesn't deserve it. He cannot accept her affection because she's loving a man who doesn't exist. He plays a role. He says he's an actor in his own home. Designed for good, my friend was sputtering and throwing smoke. The soul was not designed for this, I thought. We were supposed to be good, all of us."[15]

We were supposed to be good, but we're not. This isn't the way it's supposed to be.

The social sciences in the modern world, such as psychology and sociology, help us observe the human condition and describe the relationship between man and society. They attempt to explain how people operate. Morality, on the other hand, prescribes the way things ought to be, the way people ought to live.

C.S. Lewis says that just as physical life is governed by the law of gravity, human beings are governed by moral law—the natural moral laws he calls them. The only difference he notes is that the individual has the right to obey or not to obey.

The Christian understanding is this: The world is designed a certain way, and God imparts to each of us the way things ought to be and the way we should then live.

Dr. George Mavrodes taught philosophy at the University of Michigan for thirty-three years. He said that though the reality of moral obligations might not be proof for the existence of God, it is very strong evidence for it. He said that if anyone believes in absolute moral obligations, this only makes sense in a world where God exists. He makes it clear that this is the only way to account for one of the most significant aspects of human life. He encourages people who might not believe in God to be open to the possibility that the theistic view of life is truer to reality.[16]

Dr. Tim Keller says that, over the years, he has noticed secular people who struggle with this issue. They are not comfortable with their own point of view. He says:

> "Most of the skeptics I have seen move toward faith later told me that it was around this issue of moral obligation that they first began to wonder whether their views really fit the actual world they lived in."[17]

Dr. Robert Coles is a Pulitzer Prize-winning author, having written more than eighty books. He is both a prominent child psychiatrist and a literature professor at Harvard. He teaches literature to business majors instead of psychiatry to medical students, and the reason he gives is that we have systems to explain everything except how to live.

Coles has spent his lifetime interviewing and listening to people. What has he learned about the human condition?

> "Nothing I have discovered about the makeup of human beings contradicts in any way what I learn from the Hebrew prophets such as Isaiah, Jeremiah, and Amos, and from the book of Ecclesiastes, and from Jesus and the lives of those he touched. Anything I can say as a result of my research into human behavior is a mere footnote to those lives in the Old and New Testaments.

I have known human beings who, in the face of unbearable daily stress, respond with resilience, even nobility. And I have known others who live in a comfortable, even luxurious environment and seem utterly lost. We have both sides in all of us, and that's what the Bible says, isn't it?"[18]

Coles says that he receives a great deal of criticism from those in his profession because he speaks of human nature in terms of good and evil, light and darkness, self-destruction and redemption. He says, "They want some new theory, I suppose. But my research merely verifies what the Bible has said all along about human beings."

Coles is telling us that God has dispensed His moral law through the written word. It keeps us from moral confusion. All laws and doctrine, in order to be just and equitable, must be objective and verifiable, without being overbroad or vague. This is why laws must be recorded; they must be written down. This is how any complex society maintains moral order and coherence.

God is the moral lawgiver and has declared there is a moral order that governs life. It is revealed in the Bible. God is telling us how life should be lived. He has given us a road map so we don't get lost and a moral compass to avoid confusion. It ultimately keeps us from destroying ourselves.

I think the words that best summarize the theme of this essay come from Peter Kreeft, the great philosophy professor at Boston College, who clearly has the credentials to make a statement like this:

> "No society has ever survived or will ever survive without morality, and no morality has ever survived without a transcendent source."[19]

3.4
Morality and Science

ONE OF the most celebrated atheists in all of history was Bertrand Russell. He was highly regarded and outspoken. However, when it came to morality and value judgments, he confessed, "I don't know the solution." He placed so much confidence in science and human reason but acknowledged human impotence when it came to the issue of morality.[20]

Albert Einstein, in a discussion on science and religion back in 1930, said, "You are right in speaking of the moral foundations of science, but you cannot turn around and speak of the scientific foundations of morality." Einstein clearly believed science cannot have a basis for morality. As he put it, "Every attempt to reduce ethics to scientific formula must fail."[21]

As significant as science is to our world, it does not hold all of life's answers. It cannot determine right from wrong, because moral values lie outside of the realm of science.

I recently read a very interesting book titled *Science and the Good.* It was written by James Davison Hunter and Paul Nedelisky, both of whom are professors at the University of Virginia. It is a well-researched book examining the quest by science to find a foundation for morality. The authors were trying to determine if science could solve the enduring moral problems and fashion for modern people a good and peaceful society.

The authors examined various ways the sciences have sought to discover a universal moral code. They said:

> "Surely science can do for morality what it does for chemistry and physics—resolve differences with empirical evidence. In short,. can science demonstrate what morality is and how we should live?"[22]

The answer seems to be—no. As wonderful as science is, it is not a teacher of morals. Science cannot tell us why, scientifically, we should or should not value the enslavement of Africans. It cannot tell us scientifically why we should or should not value the purging of Jews and the mentally disabled. Science cannot tell us why, scientifically, we should permit or not permit gay marriage.[23]

What Hunter and Nedelisky have concluded is this:

> "The story of the quest for a scientific foundation for morality persuades us that the answer is no. At least, science has not gotten us there yet, there are no promising signs that it might, and no plausible solutions to the challenges this project faces.
>
> Science has taught us many things. Applied to the problems of human existence, it has brought about immeasurable benefits in health, longevity, comfort, ease of living, and security. A central part of its achievement is the immense practicality of its method and findings. It urges us to credit, and to build upon, only what can be demonstrated for all to see. Yet for all that science has taught us and for all the good that it has brought about, it has clearly not provided anything like a solution to the problem of morality—no way of resolving moral disagreement with empirical methods."[24]

So, where does that leave us? Who determines what is right and wrong, good or evil? Who has the authority and the wisdom to help us create a "good society"?

Historically, in our country, we have looked to the Judeo-Christian tradition—that is, the God of the Bible—as our source of moral authority. It is not surprising that since we as a nation have become more godless, we have morally lost our way. We have become morally confused.

This is a very important point because so many modern people believe that all truth must be sanctioned by science. Yet Hunter and Nedelisky have clearly demonstrated through their research that science is not a teacher of morals. It cannot tell us what is right and wrong with empirical scientific methods.

3.5

Moral Contradictions

OVER THE years, I have noticed the contradictory nature of atheism, particularly when it comes to morality. Many atheists have changed their minds about God and spiritual reality because their worldview is not consistent with the real world they live in. This is why Francis Schaeffer was so effective in leading young atheists away from atheism to a belief in God. He showed them how their worldview was contradictory and, therefore, incoherent.

Years ago, I paraphrased some words of G.K. Chesterton into more modern language to help people realize the contradicting nature of atheism.

> The atheist, who believes that religion is an illusion at best and a fraud at worst, should stop and take a long, hard look at the foundations of his intellectual positions. After years of reflecting upon the conflicting beliefs of atheism and theism, I have made the decision that a belief in atheism presents an insurmountable contradiction.
>
> Atheism tells me that God is dead, and therefore love is dead, morality is dead, and human life has no value. The contradiction is revealed when the atheist is not able to live a life consistent with the world he professes to believe in. A modern atheistic biology professor, for example, may complain that

> blacks in South Africa are treated as beasts, but later, in biology class, he presents the belief that men are merely sophisticated beasts, the product of an irrefutable evolutionary process. An atheistic political scientist attacks oppressive government for trampling on the inalienable rights of man, while, in the same breath, he will deny that there is a moral imperative dictated by a transcendent reality. The atheist allows that natural selection is the supreme law of nature, but then curses the fascist or the tyrant for living by the principles derived by this law.
>
> The twentieth century atheist claims that there is no such thing as love, and yet he loves. He says there is no beauty, yet he continues to be enamored by sunsets. One day he will tell you that because there is no God, there are no absolutes; therefore, justice and cruelty have no meaning. The next evening, while watching the news, he will rail against the unjust and cruel governments of the world.[25]

I think my favorite story on the contradictory nature of atheism comes from philosopher Norman Geisler. I find it to be quite humorous. He tells the story of a philosophy student in an upper-level philosophy course.

> The student wrote a research paper arguing that there is no God; consequently, he went on to argue, there can be no objective or absolute moral principles. Judged by the paper's research, scholarship, and argumentation, most would have agreed it was easily an A paper. The professor, however, wrote these words on the paper: F—I do not like this blue folder.
>
> The student stormed into the professor's office waving his paper, protesting, "This is not fair! This is totally unjust! Why should I be graded on the color of the folder? It should have been graded on its contents, not its color!"
>
> Once the student had settled down, the professor asked quietly, "Was this the paper which argued that on the basis of the godless universe in which we live, there are no objective moral principles such as fairness and justice? Did you not also

> argue that everything is a matter of one's subjective likes and dislikes?"
>
> "Yes...yes...," the student replied hesitantly.
>
> "Well then," said the professor, "I do not like blue folders. The grade will remain an F."
>
> Abruptly, the face of the young man changed. It struck him that he really did believe in objective moral principles such as fairness and justice. As the professor changed the grade to an A, the student left with a new understanding of the objective nature of morality. It is easy to proclaim that there is no God, but it is impossible to live consistently and honestly within the resulting atheistic framework.[26]

I hope you see how easy it is to proclaim there is no God, but it is quite difficult to live consistently within the resulting moral framework.

I may have first come to realize this back in the late 1960s and early 1970s, in my years of high school and college. It was a strange time, with a great deal of rebellion in my generation, yet it gave one a perfect view of the contradictory nature of moral relativism.

My generation experimented with drugs and were committed to the sexual revolution. So many young people's approach to life was articulated best by the rock star Eric Burdon: "It's my life, and I will do what I want." For that reason, so many of the rebellious truly believed that all morality was relative and subject to one's own opinion. This generation proclaimed, "I can do with my body and my life whatever I want to do." Morality was relative to whatever the person believed was best for him or her.

However, when it came to the Vietnam War, those same people believed in moral absolutes. It was a morally wrong and unjust war in their view and America should not be in it. Notice how they are now imposing their moral views on others, but how in the world could they decide what was just and unjust when they believed morality was subjective?

Friedrich Nietzsche, the philosopher who coined the phrase

"God is dead," clearly recognized the hypocrisy that existed among those who claimed to be atheists. He had great contempt for those who didn't believe in God and yet still clung to a belief in truth, morality, love, and human dignity. To Nietzsche, this hypocrisy was as great, if not greater, because of its intellectual sloppiness, than the hypocrisy he witnessed within the ranks of organized religion. The behavior of those intellectuals who believed in God was at least coherent and consistent with what they believed, and they were acting upon their beliefs.

With great courage, Nietzsche attempted to practice atheism until the day he died. As Jean-Paul Sartre said, such a life is "a cruel and long-range affair," a life where love, beauty, and meaning could not exist. Nietzsche eventually went insane, suffering from the horrors of syphilis and spending the balance of his rapidly declining life in an asylum.

Dr. Francis Schaeffer, in his book *How Should We Then Live?*, states his belief that Nietzsche lost his sanity, in part, because "he understood that insanity was the only philosophical answer if the infinite personal God does not exist." Nietzsche resided from 1881 to 1888 in the beautiful village of Silas Maria in the Swiss Engadin. This brilliant man was surrounded by some of the most beautiful scenery in the world, yet he still faced the tension and despair of atheism. As an intellectual, Nietzsche reasoned that if God is dead, then truth, beauty, and meaning must also be dead. As a human being, he cried out for meaning that can only be found in the existence of the infinite, personal God.[27]

Therein lies the great contradiction of atheism. It is an intellectually interesting argument that falls flat when confronted with reality and honesty.

It is particularly difficult to live a wise, consistent life when you have no moral compass to follow. People think all they must do is follow their hearts and desires, yet what is one to do when the heart and the desires are uncertain? We need an anchor so that we can be morally grounded. This is what the Christian worldview provides.

4.

The Search for a Meaningful Life

"What is the meaning of human life. . . ? To know an answer to this question means to be religious."

—ALBERT EINSTEIN

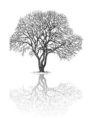

4.1

Atheism and the Meaning of Life

RICHARD DAWKINS is probably the most celebrated atheist and scientist in the world. He is the author of the best-selling book *The God Delusion.* When it comes to the issue of meaning in life, he says:

> "If the universe were just electrons and selfish genes, meaningless tragedies...are exactly what we should expect, along with equally meaningless good fortune. Such a universe we observe has precisely the properties we should expect if there is, at bottom, no design, no purpose, no evil and no good."[1]

Stephen Jay Gould of Harvard was probably the most well-known paleontologist in the world when he died several years ago. When asked about life's meaning, he responded:

> "We are here because one odd group of fishes had a peculiar fin anatomy that could transform into legs for terrestrial creatures; because comets struck the earth and wiped out dinosaurs, thereby giving mammals a chance not otherwise available (so thank your lucky stars in a literal sense); because the earth never literally froze entirely during an ice age; because a small and tenuous species, arising in Africa, a quarter of a million years ago, has managed so far to survive by hook

> and by crook. We may yearn for a higher answer—but none exists. This answer though superficially troubling, if not terrifying, is ultimately liberating and exhilarating. We cannot read the meaning of life passively in the facts of nature. We must construct these answers ourselves—from our own wisdom and ethical sense. There is no other way."[2]

David Benatar, a professor of philosophy at the University of Cape Town, came out with a book two years ago titled *The Human Predicament: A Candid Guide to Life's Biggest Questions.*

He says that life is ultimately meaningless. This is the message of evolution. It is blind and, in a cosmic sense, serves no intrinsic purpose since we each live for an insignificant amount of time. Benatar says the bottom line is that "life is terrible, and some people are unluckier than others."[3]

Each of these men offers a grim view of life because this is atheism. If there is no God, their worldview is correct and their words are true.

I first began thinking seriously about the meaning of life and the despair offered by the atheistic worldview after watching several Woody Allen films back in the 1980s. Most of his movies focus on man's search for meaning and truth. As an atheist, he has a totally pessimistic view of life, once stating publicly his belief that, after the search for truth is concluded, man is left with a real predicament:

> "… alienation, loneliness, and emptiness verging on madness. The fundamental things behind all motivation and all activity is the constant struggle against annihilation and against death. It's absolutely stupefying in its terror, and renders anyone's accomplishments meaningless."[4]

In the movie *Play It Again, Sam,* Allen plays the role of a confused divorcee. In his loneliness and insecurity, he desperately attempts to pick up women. At a museum of modern art, he approaches a lovely young woman who is admiring one of Jackson Pollock's paintings of random drippings.

> ALLEN: *"What do you see in this?"*
> WOMAN: *"It reinstates the negativeness of existence. Nothingness. The hideous lonely emptiness of the universe. The predicament of man forced to live in a godless, barren eternity like a tiny flame flickering in an immense void with nothing but waste, horror, and degradation, forming a useless bleak straight jacket in a black absurd cosmos.*
> ALLEN: *(Nodding in agreement as he looks at the painting) "What are you doing Saturday night?"*
> WOMAN: *"Committing suicide."*
> ALLEN: *"Well...what are you doing Friday night?"*

This woman's description of the Pollock painting is a true reflection of the despair found in modern atheistic philosophy. If it leads to total despair, then suicide is indeed a logical solution to be considered. It is easy for people to believe that if life has no meaning, the short existence we have on this earth will be painfully grim. Instead of having to endure it, why not simply put an end to life? Sadly, Allen numbs this bleakness with humor.

In an interview in *Newsweek* magazine, Allen said, "I still lie awake at night terrified of the void." He is speaking of the difficulty he has reconciling his strident atheism with all that he observes in the real world. Allen admits, "I make movies not to make any type of grand statement but simply to take my mind off the existential horror of being alive."[5]

As depressing as this sounds, it is the natural outworking of his godless view of life.

If you have an atheistic worldview and you logically think through its implications, you cannot help but experience despair when you consider that life is purposeless. We are here by chance, and when we die we go into everlasting nothingness. This generally culminates in a life of emptiness.

I am finding that so many modern people are like Woody Allen, who finds diversion in movie-making as a way to keep himself from having to think about all of this. Diverting the mind is much easier for us today, because of the breakneck, vastly accelerated speed of daily life. The frenzy of digital life allows so little time for introspection and reflection. We find we are subtly, insidiously encouraged to ignore the significant issues of life, particularly the issue of "meaning."

Without realizing it, we seek to divert our minds with work and pleasure, to keep us from having to think about the emptiness of life, knowing that one day this is all going to end.

4.2
Theism and the Meaning of Life

HUMAN BEINGS are driven by a deep sense of meaning and belonging. The early Greek philosophers taught that all human beings are telic creatures. "Telic" comes from the Greek word *"telos"* or *"telikós,"* which means "purpose." They believed that we are all purpose-driven, meaning-seeking creatures.

I consider them to be right. We all have to live for something in the world that makes us complete and whole, giving our lives meaning. Everyone has this yearning to feel that their lives matter, and that they will know, at the end of their lives, that what they did with their lives made a difference. We all want to have meaning, to have mattered in this world.

Viktor Frankl has written what most consider the best book on meaning in his classic best-seller *Man's Search for Meaning*. Many consider it to be one of the most influential books ever published in the United States.

Frankl was a prominent Jewish psychiatrist and neurologist who lived in Vienna, Austria. In 1942, he and his wife and parents were arrested and transported to a Nazi concentration camp. At the end of the war three years later, Frankl was set free, though his wife and parents did not survive. Following four years of recovery and reflection, Frankl spent nine days writing *Man's Search for Meaning*. In sharing his experiences in a Nazi death camp, Frankl concluded that the difference between those who had lived and those who had died came down to one thing—meaning. The reason is because he was convinced we are driven, above all, to understand our purpose in life.

This reinforced one of his key ideas:

> "Life is not primarily a quest for pleasure, as Freud believed, or a quest for power, as Alfred Adler taught, but a quest for meaning in his or her life."[6]

It is troubling when you hear modern secular people proclaim that in the final analysis, life is empty, meaningless, and without purpose. They will tell you that this is the only view that is logical in a godless universe.

However, we should all step back and ask: If this is the truth about life, why do we have this yearning for purpose and meaning?

One of my favorite writers is Philip Yancey, who says very definitely that all human beings instinctively yearn for two things. We all have a longing for meaning, a sense that our lives matter in the world we live in. We also long for a community, a sense of being loved. Why do we have this instinctive desire for meaning if it does not exist?[7]

Author Tim Keller makes a great observation about the human desire for meaning. He asks the question:

> "If there is no God, and we are just finite beings, with no intrinsic value, and when we die and go into everlasting nothingness, then why do we yearn for meaning and a sense of permanence? Where does this desire come from?"

As you look at human life, you will note that we all have certain innate desires and yearnings. It is not surprising that each of these desires has something that will satisfy it. We get hungry and thirsty, and there is food and drink to satisfy them. We have this innate desire to be productive, and there is such a thing as work to satisfy it. Every human being longs to be loved and have intimate relationships, and there is such a thing as friendship, marriage and family.

Therefore it goes to reason that if we yearn and desire for a meaningful life, a life with a sense of purpose, there must be something out there that will fulfill it.

This is clearly an indication that human beings are designed, and therefore there is a reason for our earthly existence. The Christian worldview says that God designed us and placed us here for a purpose. Therefore He is the one who guides us into a life that has meaning and purpose.

4.3

Are Your Beliefs in Harmony with Reality?

ARE YOUR beliefs in harmony with reality? Christianity and atheism offer radically different perspectives on life. They are mutually exclusive views, delivering opposite conclusions about the meaning of life and our existence as humans.

Several years ago, there was a debate held at Arizona State University. Its participants were philosopher William Lane Craig and Douglas Jesseph, a professor at North Carolina State University. The debate's topic was "Does God Exist?" The two men argued back and forth for almost ninety minutes. The crowd seemed to be evenly divided, and neither of the debaters held an upper hand until one of the final questions was posed. A student stepped up to a microphone and asked, "Can each of you tell us what difference your worldview makes to you in your own personal lives?"

Dr. Craig said that, as a philosopher (with two PhDs), he had searched in vain for meaning, for hope, and found it only when he finally came to believe in Jesus Christ. He said that Jesus changed his mind, his heart, his marriage.

"I came to know joy for the first time," he said. "I can't help but want to share the wonder of Jesus Christ whenever I am welcomed to give reason for the hope within me. I just can't keep Him to myself."

All eyes were on Professor Jesseph after Bill Craig's compelling response. He said, thoughtfully, that if he had to share his hope with someone, he wouldn't have much to say.

"I'd probably just go home, put on the Grateful Dead, and play chess with my computer."

Author Kelly Kullberg was attending the debate, and she said that after Professor Jesseph made his remarks, there was dead silence. Then several students gasped, as they understood, perhaps for the first time, that there is a connection between what one believes and the actual living of life.[8]

These students had never thought through their worldview and how it leads to certain conclusions about life. They realized that their atheistic beliefs could account for neither what they saw in the world nor what they saw in themselves, nor what they yearned for in their lives and in their future.

My experience is that younger people who claim to be atheists are like these students at Arizona State. They have never really thought through their beliefs, not realizing that if there is no God, there is no designer who stands behind our existence. Therefore, we can only conclude:

1. There is no grand purpose.
2. Life is ultimately meaningless.
3. We are alone in this vast universe.
4. When we die, we go into everlasting nothingness.

If you are honest, you have to admit this is a bleak way of looking at life. I have pointed this out about C.S. Lewis and how his atheistic worldview led to such gloom and a sense of emptiness. Becoming a Christian meant everything to him.

A week before he died, with a real peace, he declared to his brother, "I have done all that I was sent into the world to do; I am ready to go."

C.S. Lewis lived a life that was full of purpose and meaning. He had wonderful relationships and impacted the lives of many who were searching for spiritual truth. At the end of his life he was at peace, and was ready to go because he had put his hope in "the God who raises the dead."

I think it's worth repeating.

> "Christianity and atheism offer radically different perspectives on life."

The one that is true will be the one that is consistent with what you see in the real world. The one that is false will simply not be in harmony with reality.

4.4

Answering Life's Big Questions

JOHN O'NEIL has served as president of the California School of Professional Psychology and consults with chief executive officers of major corporations. He wrote the fascinating book *The Paradox of Success*. O'Neil is clearly not a man of faith, but he shares insightful words about finding meaning in life:

> "The basic questions we encounter when we look deeply into the shadow are spiritual questions. They concern our place and purpose in the world, the significance of our lives, and our personal connection to whatever force keeps the world humming along. Most of us today have moved away from the religious structures that once supplied answers to these questions, but the questions have not gone away. Our compulsive busyness, our dread of unstructured time, and our reluctance to be alone with ourselves are rooted in the uncomfortable sense that our lives lack meaning, that we are disconnected and alone."[9]

O'Neil is referring to the big questions of life, which he admits are spiritual, and they never go away. They are always confronting us. He imparts we have "moved away from the religious structures that once supplied answers to these questions." And where does that leave us? Disconnected and alone, with a life that lacks meaning.

So what are the big questions that human beings have always asked? Though there are many, I am going to limit them to three in this essay.

- Who am I?
- Why am I here?
- What is my ultimate destiny when this life is over?

When you "move away from the religious structures" to answer these questions (as O'Neil put it), you end up with no real answers. If there is no God, we are here by chance. We are nothing but a mass of molecules. A human life has no real value, for we are nothing but a product of nature. Since we are just physical beings, we have no souls or any spiritual dimension to our lives. We are meaningless beings in this random universe.

Why are we here? There is no reason for our earthly existence, because we are here by chance. Therefore, our lives are pointless, because there is no God who endowed our lives with a purpose.

Finally, when you die, your body decays and you go into everlasting nothingness. You cease to exist.

It is somewhat apparent that as we become more secular and godless, our outlook on the future becomes gloomier and more bleak, because there is no meaning in life. This explains why the depression rate is 10 times higher today than it was 50 years ago, and why suicide has surpassed car crashes as the leading cause of death due to injury.

When we go back to the three big questions, you learn that the Christian response is clearly different. It provides answers that give our earthly lives a sense of meaning and coherence.

Who are we? We are creatures designed in the image of God, which means we possess a number of God's characteristics. We possess an immortal soul, which makes us unique and of infinite value compared to animal life.

Our value as human beings is not based on what we do, what we achieve, or how successful we are. It is based clearly on the One who made us and put us here.

Why are we here? In other words, what is the reason God put us here? What is the reason of my earthly existence?

When you look at our design, it is clear that we have been given the ability to love. We are naturally relational beings. We are told:

> ". . . all things have been created by Him and for Him." (Colossians 1:16)
>
> ". . . we exist for Him . . ." (I Corinthians 8:6)

God put us here to connect with Him, to have a relationship with Him, to know Him and to love Him.

When you think about it, it is similar to why we have children. We bring children into the world, anticipating a loving lifelong relationship with them. This is what God anticipates with us.

Finally, ***what is my ultimate destiny once this life ends? Is there life after this life?***

The main theme of the Bible is the answer to this question. If you read the four Gospels in the New Testament, you will notice two phrases that Jesus uses over and over. These phrases are:

Eternal life

The Kingdom of God

Notice that Jesus places special emphasis on the importance of obtaining eternal life and entering the Kingdom of God.

He makes it obvious that you enter through Him. He is the door. He is the way. As we put our faith in Him, we are allowed to enter.

So, what is our final destiny?

Eternal life in the Kingdom of God through Jesus Christ.

These are the answers to life's big questions. Christianity answers them all. This is why the Christian faith gives such coherence to this life, as it provides the path to a meaningful life, and hope as we look to the future and the end of our earthly life.

4.5

Harvard: Our Culture in Microcosm

IN THIS essay, I hope to help you glean some insight into the emptiness of modern life.

First of all, it is essential to understand the word "microcosm." The simplest definition is "something that is seen as a small version of something much larger." Through this one concept, I hope to illustrate how Harvard University, the great educational institution, is a small version of what is happening in Western culture.

In addition, I must declare that I have no ax to grind with Harvard. I stumbled upon this idea from two books I read. The first was *The Question of God* by the late Dr. Armand Nicholi, who was a professor of psychiatry at Harvard Medical School and also taught a popular undergraduate-level course at Harvard for 35 years. The second book was *Finding God Beyond Harvard* by Kelly Kullberg, founder of the Veritas Forum at Harvard, where she served as a chaplain to students.

Harvard was founded in 1636, and one of its central bylaws was this:

> "Let every student be earnestly pressed to consider well that the main end of his life and studies is to know God and Jesus Christ who is eternal life–and therefore to lay Christ in the

> bottom, as the only foundation of all sound knowledge and learning."

There is no doubt that Harvard was a spiritually vibrant place for years. In fact, various groups and individuals believe this was the foundation that led to its initial greatness as an educational institution.

That has all changed. It appears today that Jesus has been expelled from the institution. When Henri Nouwen resigned from Harvard Divinity School in 1985, he described the place as a spiritual desert, that God was dead at Harvard, even at the divinity school.

In February of 1993, American Christian evangelist Billy Graham conducted a lengthy meeting with Harvard's president, Derek Bok. As Graham was leaving, he asked Bok one last question, "What is the number one struggle the students at Harvard have to contend with?" Bok had no need to give it much thought, as he quickly responded, "Living with emptiness."[10]

Upon hearing this, Kullberg asked the question, "How did such a great institution like Harvard become a place of emptiness?"

Kullberg shares a shocking incident upon attempting to reach out and minister to a few of the women at Harvard Divinity School. She attended a women's meeting that was held in the University Chapel, called "The Full Moon Circle." The group described themselves as a Neo-pagan, pre-Christian, ecofeminist Wiccan society. Of course, Wiccan societies practice witchcraft.

Kullberg describes the chapel as packed. The women chanted to the spirits, worshipped the full moon, and attempted to reach their dead ancestors. It was shocking to see these bright, educated women acting as if they were unenlightened pagans.[11]

In 2006, the cover story of Harvard's student newspaper, *The Crimson,* revealed the rampant incidence of student depression among the university's 6,700 students. The newspaper reported that 80 percent of the student body had experienced depression at least once during the school year. Nearly half (47 percent) of the student body found themselves depressed to the point of having a hard time functioning. Ten percent (650 students) had strongly considered committing suicide.[12]

Nobel Prize-winning French novelist Albert Camus said, "There is but one truly philosophical problem, and that is suicide. Judging whether life is worth living amounts to answering the fundamental question of philosophy." Camus knew of many people who took their lives because they saw life to be meaningless and, therefore, not worth living.[13]

Thomas Masaryk, the first president of liberated Czechoslovakia after World War I, wrote the book *Suicide and the Meaning of Civilization.* The thesis of the book states that the more godless a society becomes, the higher the rate of suicide. His research suggests that in the Middle Ages, the number of suicides was negligible. By the end of the nineteenth century, suicide had become one of the top causes of death. Today, suicide has surpassed car crashes as the leading cause of death due to injury. Furthermore, Masaryk uncovered that the vast majority of these deaths occurred among highly principled, well-educated people who had no religious faith. His conclusion reveals the tragic story of those individuals who can find no purpose in life and, therefore, have no reason to live.[14]

To acquire meaning, you have to look to God to answer life's significant questions. These concern our place and purpose in the world, the significance of our lives, and our ultimate destiny. Unfortunately, much of our population has moved away from the biblical worldview that has always supplied the answers. But, the questions have not gone away and they never will. Modern man is therefore left all alone, disconnected from the One who gives life meaning.

4.6

How Albert Camus Changed His Mind

I REMEMBER in my freshman year in college, back in the 1970s, in an introductory philosophy class, one of the required books to read was Albert Camus' *The Stranger.* I recently listened to a sermon by Tim Keller, and he said that when he was a college student in the 1960s, he took a course where Camus's book *The Myth of Sisyphus* was required reading. Author and scholar Nancy Pearcey studied in Germany in the 1970s. She said existentialism was wildly popular among university students in Europe. She said all of her classmates were avid readers of Albert Camus. Clearly, he was quite the popular author on college campuses during these turbulent times, and his philosophy filtered down and shaped the lives of many of these young people.

Albert Camus was a French philosopher, author, and journalist. He won the Nobel Prize in literature in 1957, but not for any particular work, because the award is based on the author's body of work as a whole. He was truly a celebrity figure, with a huge following on college campuses where he would often go and lecture.

Camus is considered by many to be an existential philosopher because most of his philosophy focused on existential questions. His atheistic worldview caused him to explore what he called "the absurdity of life." He considered life to be absurd because it was void of meaning, and it is void of meaning because there is no God to give it meaning. He also argued that human life is rendered meaningless because of death, which prevents anyone to make sense of their earthly existence.[15]

Camus believed there was no God, no meaning, and therefore we create our own meaning by throwing ourselves into life and challenging the futility of our earthly existence. It seems Camus never could shake the issue of meaning, which he realized was life's most fundamental issue.

What most people don't know is that Albert Camus had a change of heart the year before he was killed in a car crash.

Howard Mumma was a Methodist minister in the United States. For several years, he would spend the summer in Paris preaching at an English-speaking church. One Sunday morning, he noticed that the celebrated philosopher Albert Camus was sitting in one of the pews. They met and struck up a friendship. Camus clearly was searching for answers, and he now seemed to realize that meaning and purpose has to be endowed by God.

The conversation below is from Howard Mumma's book *Albert Camus and the Minister.*

It begins with Mumma speaking to Camus:

MUMMA: *You have said to me again and again that you're dissatisfied with the whole philosophy of existentialism and that you are privately seeking something that you do not have.*

CAMUS: *Yes, you are exactly right, Howard. The reason I have been coming to church is because I am seeking. I'm almost on a pilgrimage—seeking something to fill the void that I am experiencing—and no one else knows. Certainly, the public and the readers of my novels, while they see that void, are not finding the answers in what they are reading. But deep down, you are right—I am searching for something that the world is not giving me.*

MUMMA: *Albert, I congratulate you for this. I think that I want to encourage you to keep searching for a meaning and something that will fill the void and transform your life. Then you will arrive in living waters where you will find meaning and purpose.*

CAMUS: *Well, Howard, you have to agree that in a sense we are all products of a mundane world, a world without spirit. The world in which we live and the lives which we live are decidedly empty.*

MUMMA: *It does often seem that way, I concede.*

CAMUS: *Since I have been coming to church, I have been thinking a great deal about the idea of a transcendent, something that is other than this world. It is something that you do not hear much about today, but I am finding it. I am hearing about it here, in Paris, within the walls of the American Church. After all, one of the basic teachings that I learned from Sartre is that man is alone. We are solitary centers of the universe. Perhaps we ourselves are the only ones who have ever asked the great questions of life. Perhaps, since Nazism, we are also the ones who have loved and lost and who are, therefore, fearful of life. That is what led us to existentialism. And since I have been reading the Bible, I sense that there is something—I don't know if it is personal or if it is a great idea or powerful influence—but there is something that can bring meaning to my life. I certainly don't have it, but it is there. On Sunday mornings, I hear that the answer is God.*[16]

At the very end of the book, Mumma is explaining to Camus God's forgiveness of sins and the necessity to have your slate washed clean in order to have a relationship with God. Mumma then says:

> "I don't know what the French term would be for a bond or an encumbrance, but the person who accepts forgiveness now believes that there is no mortgage, no encumbrance on you. The slate is clear, your conscience is clear. You are ready to move ahead and commit yourself to a new life, a new spiritual pilgrimage. You are seeking the presence of God Himself."

I was nervous and intense. Albert looked me squarely in the eye and with tears in his eyes, said,

> "Howard, I am ready. I want this. This is what I want to commit my life to."[17]

This was in the summer of 1959, just before Mumma returned to the States. Camus met the minister at the airport, and as he was about to board the plane they hugged and Camus said to Mumma, "My friend, mon cheri, thank you...I am going to keep striving for the Faith."[18]

Four months later, on January 4, 1960, Albert Camus died in a car crash. At the time, he was one of the most famous Frenchmen alive. He had a huge following. However, most of them never knew, nor probably would believe, that he turned from the meaninglessness of atheism to a life of purpose that is found in Christ.

Albert Camus reveled early in his life as a famous and celebrated atheistic author and speaker. He had a great following of young people who fully embraced his teaching on "the absurdity of life." As I read Mumma's book it struck me that Camus found his atheistic worldview to be unlivable. He could not live with his belief that life is ultimately empty, meaningless, and absurd. He recognized he had this deep thirst for meaning, and had the courage and the humility to be willing to abandon the atheistic philosophy that made him famous and begin a search for the truth. His search led him to God.

5.

The Human Experience

When you have an atheist's worldview, you are building your life upon a "firm foundation of unyielding despair."

—BERTRAND RUSSELL

5.1

The Mystery of Love

DR. VIKTOR Frankl spent three years of his life in Nazi concentration camps, and one great truth he recognized from that experience is that love is the ultimate and highest goal to which all humans aspire. To love and be loved is the deepest of all yearnings of the human heart. Love transforms us, and it is not surprising that we experience the greatest joy in this life when we love.[1]

But where does love fit in a world where God does not exist? If we are nothing but material beings composed of a mass of particles, then what is love to us? Atheistic philosophy readily admits that love has no meaning in our lives other than its pragmatic, physical consequences. As B.F. Skinner concluded, love is an illusion.

Similarly, Jean-Paul Sartre painted a very bleak picture of love. In his book *Nausea,* Sartre gives life to a character named Roquentin, who spoke of his disgust at the way in which a man and a woman are behaving toward one another. Roquentin's disgust stems from his belief of the absurdity of love in a godless universe.

Aldous Huxley was even more critical of the idea of love.

> "Of all the worn, smudged, dog-eared words in our vocabulary, love is surely the grubbiest, smelliest, slimiest. Bawled

> from a million pulpits, lasciviously crooned through hundreds of loud speakers, it has become an outrage to good taste and decent feeling, an obscenity which one hesitates to pronounce."[2]

Harvard psychologist Daniel Wegner says that having a free will to love someone else is an illusion because all of our actions and feelings, including love, are the effects of unconscious physical causes.

One of the discoverers of DNA was Dr. Francis Crick, an atheist. He believed all the joys of life are no more than "the behavior of a vast assembly of nerve cells and their associated molecules." Therefore, you are nothing more than a molecule machine and the love you think you are experiencing is only a biological reaction.[3]

C.S. Lewis described the atheistic view of love in these words:

> "The universe is a universe of nonsense, but since you are here, grab what you can. Unfortunately...you can't, except in the lowest animal sense, be in love with a girl if you know (and keep on remembering) that all the beauties both of her person and of her character are a momentary and accidental pattern produced by the collision of atoms, and that your own response to them is only a sort of psychic phosphorescence arising from the behavior of your genes."[4]

Secular psychologists explain away the love we believe we are experiencing as a result of natural selection and as a calculated strategy of giving and serving someone else so that they might give and serve you in return. Love is therefore a strategy of "reciprocal altruism" so that we will get along and survive better. As Nancy Pearcey says,

> "The assumption is that individuals practice cooperation and self-control only when it secures their larger interests. Every good deed is ultimately selfish."[5]

This is the atheistic view of love. It makes you wonder how anyone could come up with this view when it is so contrary to what we experience in everyday life.

Dr. Francis Schaeffer, philosopher, scholar, and author of several seminal books, introduces us to the parable of the two young lovers on the Left Bank of Paris who fall in love and then weep because they do not believe that love truly exists. Schaeffer goes on to describe what he would say to these young lovers if he were to meet them:

> "At this moment you understand something real about the universe. Though your system may say love does not exist, your own experience shows that it does. Though these youngsters do not believe in a personal God, for a fleeting moment, they have touched the existence of true personality in their love. This indeed is an objective reality, and no mere illusion."[6]

Susan Macaulay, in her book *How to Be Your Own Selfish Pig*, shares the true story of Philippe and Françoise, two bright and sophisticated students at the Sorbonne University in Paris. One day the two meet, romance blossoms, and they begin living together during the school year.

When their studies end, the lovers are perplexed over what to do next. It is more convenient for them to separate, so they part and go their separate ways.

Philippe tries to push aside his feelings for Françoise by employing the concepts he learned in his philosophy classes at school. *Love is an illusion,* he reasons. *These feelings I have are temporary and are a result of my hormones. Other women will come along to replace Françoise.*

As the months go by, Philippe and Françoise cannot forget each other. The sexual relationships they experience with others seem empty. They pursue lives that they believe will provide them with excitement and satisfaction, but find that the theory they believe in is not working for them. They finally come back together.

Mrs. McCaulay first met Philippe at L'Abri School in Switzerland, where his confusion eventually led him. Philippe could not understand why it was so difficult to live without genuine love and commitment. He acknowledged that he never realized how his atheistic ideas about life were draining it of its joy:

> "I have always believed that the human being was the result of chance. We are like machines doing what we are programmed to do by our genes and instincts and hormones. This means that I cannot make choices; my genetic program is running me. I cannot really love. A computer can't love! Beauty has no meaning. Love relationships are a farce, an illusion!"[7]

For Philippe, life did not have any meaning or joy, and consequently led only to confusion. What he believed to be true intellectually contradicted what he felt to be true *experientially*.

One of the most interesting personal stories I have read is the life of journalist and author A.N. Wilson. Many thought he might become the next C.S. Lewis, until he renounced his faith. Richard Dawkins and Christopher Hitchens were thrilled to see their friend come back to atheism. He spent many years mocking Christianity. Then something very strange happened that stunned many of his followers: He returned to the Christian faith.

In an interview with "New Statesman," in explaining his reasons for coming back to the Christian faith, he said that atheists "are missing out on some very basic experiences of life." Wilson clearly recognized that the Christian "perception of life was deeper, wiser, and more rounded than my own."

He concluded that those people who insist we are "simply anthropoid" apes cannot account for the basic experiences of life, particularly love. He also observed how Christian faith transforms people's individual lives, and it convinced Wilson the Christian faith is simply true.[8]

Do you recognize love to be a reality in your life and relationships? If you are an atheist and believe in love, do you not recognize the massive contradiction in your life? Love cannot exist other than some type of chemical response in your brain because we, in the final analysis, are nothing but atoms and molecules in motion with no purpose.

The worldview that clearly supports the highest aspirations of love is Christianity. It recognizes love to be real because God is the source of that love. As the apostle John said: "Love is from God" and "We love because He first loved us." Atheism clearly denies the mystery of love.

This entire essay can be summarized in these powerful words of author and scholar Nancy Pearcey:

> "Love is not an illusion created by the genes to promote our evolutionary survival, but an aspect of human nature that reflects the fundamental fabric of ultimate reality."[9]

5.2

The Question of Beauty

I REMEMBER a number of years ago driving down a highway at the end of the day. A magnificent sunset was unfolding, and then the radio station began to play my very favorite song from college, "Stairway to Heaven" by Led Zeppelin. A powerful euphoric feeling came upon me as this beautiful visual sunset and this wonderful song converged. It was a brief experience that I have never forgotten. I have reflected on that moment from time to time and have concluded that it was the visual beauty of the sunset and the audio beauty of the song that moved me so powerfully.

But what is beauty? How do you define it? It strikes me that beauty is quickly realized by the one who beholds it. We know there is something special about it because it moves us. It stirs us. We experience it deep from within.

C.S. Lewis would tell you it is a clue to the meaning of the universe. He would tell you that beauty in this world is a sign that points you to something significant. The human quest for true beauty is the central theme of his wonderful short work *The Weight of Glory.* Lewis was convinced that we all possess an instinct for transcendence that is stimulated by beauty.

Alister McGrath, I believe, provides some profound insight when he said, "The human quest for beauty is thus really a quest for the source of that beauty. However, it is not contained in this world."[10]

What do we make of beauty if there is no God, and we are nothing but chemicals and molecules? Richard Dawkins, in his best-selling book *The God Delusion,* is quite blunt about it: "Beauty is just a chemical reaction."[11]

Before becoming a Christian, C.S. Lewis agreed with Dawkins. He believed that all reality was:

> "a meaningless dance of atoms and that any suggestion of beauty within nature was simply a subjective phosphorescence." At this particular stage he believed his atheistic worldview was true, though he conceded that it offered a "grim and meaningless" view of life.[12]

Later in his life as a Christian, he looked back on his former worldview and said this:

> "You can't get much pleasure from beautiful music if you believe its beauty is 'pure illusion' and that the only reason you find it appealing is 'because your nervous system is irrationally conditioned to like it.' He said you may enjoy the music but 'you will be forced to feel the hopeless disharmony between your own emotions and the universe in which you [think you] really live.'"[13]

I believe Nancy Pearcey has articulated it best:

> "The naturalist asserted that the universe does not have an author, and therefore things do not have a secondary, higher meaning. Humans are trapped in a one-dimensional world of sheer biological existence. Nature is 'red in tooth and claw.' Life is a harsh, dog-eat-dog struggle for survival. This was a dark, gloomy picture of the world, and many naturalists responded by dismissing the very concept of beauty. 'The time

> for Beauty is over,' Flaubert stated bluntly. The public has a hard time understanding why many modern artists have rejected the ideal of beauty. But it is understandable when we realize that it was a consequence of a ruthless naturalistic worldview. Works by naturalist writers typically featured sordid settings, violent plots, coarse characters, and language laced with slang and obscenities."[14]

When you reduce the world to nothing but matter, you risk losing your sense of wonder and appreciation for beauty. You drain all the joy out of life. You see this is what took place in the life of Charles Darwin. These are his own words from his autobiography:

> "Up to the age of thirty or beyond it, poetry of many kinds... gave me great pleasure, and even as a schoolboy I took intense delight in Shakespeare...Formerly pictures gave me considerable, and music very great, delight. But now for many years I cannot endure to read a line of poetry: I have tried to read Shakespeare, and found it so intolerably dull that it nauseated me. I have almost lost any taste for pictures or music...I retain some taste for fine scenery, but it does not cause me the exquisite delight which it formerly did...My mind seems to have become a kind of machine for grinding general laws out of a large collection of facts...The loss of these tastes is a loss of happiness, and may possibly be injurious to the intellect, and more probably to the moral character, by enfeebling the emotional part of our nature."[15]

It appears that Darwin is acknowledging that his loss of happiness is a result of his change in worldview. His naturalistic perspective over time undermined his appreciation for beauty, resulting in a joyless, unhappy life.

So, we must consider this question: If there is no God, how do we account for all the joy and beauty we experience in this life? Have you ever been moved by a star-lit sky, the beauty of the ocean, or some other body of water? Then you have the view from the top of a mountain, along with a gorgeous sunset. Do any of these have any evolutionary or survival value? Beauty is a reality, but how do you account for it?

The argument for beauty works like the argument for morality and human love. Atheism does not appear to have a plausible explanation for the human appreciation for beauty, and therefore concludes that it is an illusion. However, it is difficult to accept this conclusion when we continually encounter beauty that moves us in such a powerful way.

5.3

On Death and Dying

THE PAGAN Greek philosopher Epicurus, who lived three hundred years before Christ, believed that all people should be liberated from a belief in God, the immortal soul, and the afterlife. Epicurus would have us believe that such an enlightened philosophical understanding would make it easier to live in the present.

Yet even Epicurus himself seemed to be tormented by the possibility that he might be wrong. He wrote:

> "If we could be sure that death was annihilation, then there would be no fear of it. For as long as we exist, death is not there, and when it does come, we no longer exist. But we cannot be totally sure there is annihilation, for what people fear most is not that maybe death is annihilation, but that maybe death is not."[16]

It strikes me that if atheists feel certain about what they believe, then there should be a confidence that death is nothing more than the cessation of life. What is to fear if you go into everlasting nothingness?

However, Epicurus realized he could not say this with certainty because he admitted no one can be sure of what lies beyond the grave. We as humans always seem to be drawn back to this question: "If a person dies, will they live again?"

A number of years ago I wrote a book titled *Safe Passage: Thinking Clearly About Life and Death.* In my research I discovered that many atheists struggled mightily with their godless worldview as they approached death.

Freud was conflicted with what he called "the terrors of eternal nothingness." One would expect Sigmund Freud, the father of psychoanalysis, to have had a good grip on the nature and causes of human psychological weakness in the face of death, but he lived with a dreadful fear of death throughout his life. In one of his letters he complained, "As for me, I note migraine, nasal secretion, and attacks of fear of dying."

Ernest Jones has written a comprehensive biography of Freud's life, and he points out:

> "Freud seems to have been prepossessed with thoughts about death, more so than any other great man I can think of. He hated growing old, even as early as in his forties, and as he did so, the thoughts of death became increasingly clamorous. He once said he thought of it every day of his life."[17]

The famous French philosopher Voltaire was a confident atheist all of his life, once saying, "I am of the opinion that one ought never to think of death—death is a mere nothing." In two separate books I read that he cried out on his deathbed, "I must die, abandoned of God and of men." He apparently was terrified.[18]

The famous philosopher Bertrand Russell was an outspoken atheist all of his life. He once made this comment: "There is darkness without, and when I die there will be darkness within." On another occasion he was quoted as saying, "When I die, I rot."

However, Donald Coggan, former archbishop of Canterbury, in his book *The Heart of the Christian Faith,* reveals that a close friend of his was with Bertrand Russell as Russell lay on his deathbed. Coggan informs us that Russell asked his friend, a Christian layman, to pray with him. It appears that at the end of his life, Bertrand Russell had lost his faith in atheism.[19]

Even the godless tyrant Joseph Stalin could not seem to shake the presence of God. *Newsweek* magazine quoted his daughter, Svetlana:

> "My father died a difficult and terrible death…God grants an easy death only to the just…At what seemed the very last moment he suddenly opened his eyes and cast a glance over everyone in the room. It was a terrible glance, insane or perhaps angry and full of fear of death…then he lifted his left hand as though he were pointing to something above and bringing down a curse on us all. The gesture was full of menace…The next moment…the spirit wrenched itself free of the flesh."[20]

She later said it was as if he was shaking his fist at God, in one final act of defiance.

In an earlier essay I wrote about Albert Camus recanting his atheistic belief—assuredly a most fascinating turn of events. Camus was friends with one of the most influential atheists ever to live, Jean-Paul Sartre. I remember reading about Sartre's death in 1980 and while researching this book, I discovered that Sartre also seems to have abandoned atheism at the end of his life.

Thirty days before he died, he shared these words in a published interview:

> "The world seems ugly, bad and without hope. There, that's the cry of despair of an old man who will die in despair. But that's exactly what I resist. I know that I shall die in hope… the only problem is…hope, faith needs a foundation."[21]

Sartre seemed to be searching for faith but recognized faith and belief must have a foundation to undergird it; otherwise it is blind faith. He was looking for a reason to believe. Sartre's good friend Pierre Victor is the one who revealed that Sartre had recanted his atheism just before he died. Victor spent a great deal of time with Sartre during the last days of his life. He said that

Sartre "had a drastic change of mind about the existence of God." According to Victor, Sartre said, "I do not feel that I am a product of chance, a speck of dust in the universe, but someone who was expected, prepared, prefigured. In short, a being whom only a Creator could put here." In the end, it seems quite clear that atheism for Jean-Paul Sartre was unlivable.[22]

Apparently, even Charles Darwin struggled with his belief in God, and it impacted his perspective on death and dying. He refused to be called an atheist, insisting that he was agnostic, meaning he was not certain what he believed. For years he kept a letter written to him by his wife, Emma. She was a committed Christian, and her letter implored him not to turn away from Christ for fear of them being eternally separated from one another. On Easter of 1881 Darwin tearfully wrote these words: "When I am dead, know that many times I have kissed and cried over this." Darwin never seemed to be able to come to terms with his belief in God. He died a year later in April of 1882 in the arms of his beloved wife.[23]

Clearly, the process of coming to terms with our mortality is very painful. As psychiatrist Armand Nicholi has observed,

"The unbelievable brevity of our lives conflicts with our deep-seated yearning for permanence and with our lifelong fear of being separated from those we love, a fear that haunts us from infancy to old age."[24]

The Christian worldview, however, seeks to deliver us from this fear.

Dr. David Nelson, a 19th-century physician, sat at the bedside of many of his patients as they lay dying. He wrote about those experiences. He looked into the faces of the terminally ill patients and watched many of them die with no religious faith, and they would try and keep a brave face on their terror. Nelson said, "I could see the fear in their countenance, and it was quite chilling." He saw many people "die cowardly deaths."

Nelson, who for many years did not believe in God, witnessed the death of many Christians as well. As he looked into their faces, he noted a sense of tranquility. He wrote, "I beheld more celestial triumph than I had ever witnessed anywhere else. In their voice there was a sweetness, and in their eye was a glory that I never would have believed if I had not been there to see it."

David Nelson eventually came to a strong faith in Christ, in part because he saw the reality of Jesus in the lives of those dying Christians.[25]

One of the foundations of the Christian faith is that Christ abolished death. We are told that one of the reasons He came into the world is to set people free from the fear of death; otherwise they will be slaves to this fear all of their lives (Hebrews 2:15). Jesus has given us these words to trust: "I am the Resurrection and the life. He who believes in Me will live even if he dies." A few days later, Christ validated these words by rising from the dead and demonstrating His power over death.

This leads us back to Epicurus' logic. Maybe what people fear most is not that Jesus failed to rise from the dead, but maybe he did. And if He did indeed rise from the dead, what exactly would that mean? Well it would mean **everything.**

It would mean Jesus is who He said He was and is the living proof that legitimizes His claims to deity. Furthermore, it would mean that Jesus' words and the example of His life has the authority and power to teach us what is true about death and eternity. If we sincerely believe that Jesus' life and experience and voice is trustworthy, we should then have every right to expect that when God's everlasting kingdom becomes accessible to us, it will indeed be more wonderful than anything we could imagine.

This is the heart of Pascal's great wager. He said that every person on the face of the earth is making a high-stakes, life commitment to a particular faith view of God. You are betting your view is right.

5.4

Human Sexuality

WE HAVE been considering life from the two predominant worldviews in our land: Christianity and Atheism. These two worldviews clearly do not agree on where life comes from, what life means, or what we as humans should be doing during the few allotted years that we have on earth. They do not agree on what motivates our actions.

One of the most emotional and divisive issues in Western society is that of human sexuality. At the root of this moral issue is this question: Are we merely products of nature, or does the world we live in reflect some type of purpose that has been bestowed on us by God?

As scholar Nancy Pearcey declares,

> "A society's worldview ultimately determines whether it treats the human body as another piece of matter or whether it grants the body value and dignity, imbuing sexual relations with the depth and significance we all long for."[26]

Clearly our societies' secular view of sex is a reflection of its prevailing worldview. If our world is a product of blind, material forces, then there are no rules for sex. Therefore, it means we are free to make our own rules. It means that sex can be just another form of recreation; it is for pleasure. In our secular worldview, our culture has no God to instruct us how to limit our lusts, our passions, and our desires. This explains how sex in our modern world has no real meaning or value. There is nothing sacred about it.

The most prominent sexologist in modern times was a man by the name of Alfred Kinsey. He was a biologist and sexologist who founded The Institute for Sex Research at Indiana University. His research on human sexuality is extensive. A 2004 movie on his life's work, *Kinsey*, stars prominent actor Liam Neeson.

Kinsey was a pure secularist, and therefore there was no place for God in his research. His view was that, as a mammal, you should be able to enjoy sex with any other mammal of your choosing. This could include your mother, uncle, sister, or even an animal. While this might sound extreme, sound reason alone would have to agree with Kinsey. As the Russian author Fyodor Dostoevsky rightly stated, "If there is no God, all things are permissible." This would include human sexuality[27]

In our modern secular culture, there is a great deal of freedom when it comes to sexual activity because each individual decides what is moral or immoral for themselves. We set our own boundaries.

The Christian worldview contends that the healthiest, most meaningful, most satisfying, and most pleasurable sexual experience is found between a man and a woman in a covenant relationship called marriage. A covenant is a promise—a pledge of love, loyalty, and faithfulness. A covenant involves continuity—the sense of a common future—to look forward to and a history to look back on together. A covenant means belonging—a commitment to a rich and growing relationship of love and care.

In Matthew 19:5, Jesus says from the Old Testament, "A man shall leave his father and mother and cleave to his wife, and the two shall become one flesh."

The word 'cleave' is a Hebrew word that means absolute unity. Total union. Deep, profound solidarity. Not just a physical union but an emotional union, an economic union, a social union. A complete union. To cleave to someone is to say, "I belong exclusively to you. Permanently. Everything I have is yours. I am yours."

This is what marriage is. This is why God created sex—for cleaving. Sex is a cleaving apparatus.

Furthermore, there is a deep longing in our hearts for a deep connection with someone else. God created sex to help us deal with loneliness by giving us a deep connection with our spouse. It helps us to be truly known and completely vulnerable to someone else.

God made sex to be able to say to one other human being, I belong completely, and exclusively, and permanently, to you. All of me. Everything. Most followers of the traditional Christian view of sexuality believe that it is sacred, beautiful, meaningful.[28]

Four years ago, I wrote a book titled *Sex at First Sight.* It was about the modern hookup culture. From my research, it is quite clear that the Christian view of sex is healthier, more pleasurable, and more meaningful than the secular view. The evidence is overwhelming.

In October of 2017 there was an article in *The New York Times* on the exploding rates of sexually transmitted diseases. The article indicated that at any given time, there are an estimated 110 million sexually transmitted infections in the United States. Dr. Gail Bolan, Director of the Division of Sexually Transmitted Disease Prevention at The Centers for Disease Control, describes it as "epidemic."[29]

Have you ever stopped and considered the number of destructive problems we have because of the misuse of our sexuality? Not only do we have an epidemic of sexually transmitted diseases, but addiction to pornography is exploding and causing all types of problems in relationships. In many cases it is ruining people's marriages and sex lives. Then there are so many unwanted pregnancies, which lead to abortions. There are all types of psychological and physical effects from rape, sexual abuse, sexual harrassment, incest, sex trafficking of young girls, prostitution, and all the different types of sexual addictions. Finally, and most significantly, there is adultery, which often leads to divorce and the break-up of the family. It appears that sex is out of control and causing far-reaching damage to our society.

The National Survey of Counseling Directors conducted a study, interviewing 6,500 adolescents. All 6,500 were sexually active teenage girls. They learned that sexually active teenage girls are three times more likely to be depressed and nearly three times as likely to attempt suicide as young women who are not sexually active.[30]

The National Health and Social Life Council completed the most extensive survey of Americans' sex lives ever. They found sexually active singles have the most sexual problems and get the least pleasure out of sex. Married couples by far reported the happiest and most satisfaction in their sex lives. Surprisingly, the most satisfied demographic group is that of married couples between fifty and fifty-nine. It would appear that when you are committed to someone over a period of years, your sex life gets better over time.[31]

One of the best-selling books on sexual freedom and sexual liberation in the last fifty years was *Open Marriage: A New Lifestyle for Couples* by anthropologists Nena and George O'Neill. In one sense, they approved of hookup sex for married couples, believing that you should be allowed to engage freely in extramarital sex with whomever you please. The O'Neills believed that the Judeo-Christian traditional marriage system was outdated. Yet, five years after the book became a national bestseller, Nena O'Neill completely changed her mind. So many of the couples they spoke with who experimented with consensual adultery found the results to be disastrous. She recognized there is a price to pay for unrestrained sexual activity.[32]

George Leonard is an American author and educator who died in 2010. He wrote fifteen books and at one time was editor of *Look Magazine.* For a number of years, Leonard was a big proponent of the sexual liberation movement. He believed in complete sexual freedom—that one should enjoy sex with multiple partners. At the time, he would have been a real advocate of the hookup culture. But years later, Leonard wrote a book ironically titled *The End of Sex: Erotic Love after the Sexual Revolution.* Leonard says,

> "I have finally come to see that every game has a rule, and sex has rules. Unless you play by the rules, you'll find sex can create a depth of loneliness that nothing else can."

If Leonard's observation is correct, that sex has rules and ignoring these rules leads to painful consequences, then one must ask two simple questions: What are the rules, and who makes them?[33]

Personally, I think it starts with God because sex was His idea. And it seems only logical that if sex is God's idea, He must have a blueprint that leads to the ultimate sexual experience.

It's interesting that even liberal feminist Naomi Wolf believes the new sexuality is having a devastating impact on young women. She says,

> "The message young women heard was 'just go for it' sexually…We have raised a generation of young women, and men, who don't understand sexual ethics. They don't see sex as sacred or even very important anymore. Sex has been commodified and drained of its deeper meaning."[34]

She is correct. Sex has become a commodity. For so many people, sex is reduced to an exchange of bodily pleasure between two people, and the resulting mentality is that, "I am not in this relationship for you but in it for what I can get from you. You are nothing but an object whose purpose is to give me pleasure."

Finally, I stumbled upon a most curious study from 1934. Prominent scholar J.D. Unwin published several books, including *Sex and Culture.* To complete this book, Unwin spent many years closely studying 86 civilizations. His findings startled many people, including Unwin himself, as all 86 demonstrated a direct tie between absolute heterosexual monogamy and the "expansive energy" of civilization. In other words, sexual fidelity was the single most important predictor of a society's ascendancy and strength.

Unwin carried no religious convictions and applied no moral judgment.

> "I offer no opinion about rightness or wrongness," Unwin said. "In human records there is no instance of a society retaining its energy after a completely new generation has inherited a tradition which does not insist on pre-nuptial sexual restraint."

He stated emphatically that without a doubt, civilizations flourish when demonstrating premarital sexual restraint, faithfulness, and fidelity in marriage. From Roman, Greek, Sumerian, Moorish, Babylonian, and Anglo-Saxon civilizations, Unwin studied hundreds of years of history to draw upon, finding no exceptions. These societies flourished culturally and geographically during eras that valued sexual fidelity. Inevitably, sexual standards would loosen, and the societies would subsequently decline, only to rise again when they returned to the more rigid sexual standards.

Unwin seemed at a loss to explain the pattern.

> "If you ask me why this is so," Unwin comments, "I reply that I do not know. No scientist does...You can describe the process and observe it, but you cannot explain it."[35]

After reading Unwin's book, Christian author Philip Yancey offered this:

> "Unwin preached a message that few people want to hear. Without realizing it, though, Unwin may have subtly edged toward a Christian view of sexuality from which modern society has badly strayed. For the Christian, sex is not an end

> in itself, but rather a gift from God. Like such gifts, it must be stewarded according to God's rules, not ours."[36]

Christianity teaches that there is a divinely established moral order, and we, as human beings, just cannot decide for ourselves what is moral. When we choose to defy God's moral order, there is a price we must pay.

5.5

Our Never-Ending Pursuit of Happiness

IN FEBRUARY of 2018 there was an article in *The New York Times* about Yale University and a psychology course being offered there. This class has become the most popular class that has ever been offered at Yale. Nearly one-fourth of Yale undergraduates are enrolled in this class. The course tries to teach students how to lead a happier, more satisfying life. According to Laurie Santos, the professor who teaches the course, "there is a serious mental health crisis among the students." A 2013 report by the Yale College Council found that more than half of undergraduates sought mental health care from the university during their time of enrollment.[37]

This is not surprising because, in the same year, the World Health Organization announced that depression has become the most widespread illness in the world, and the numbers are rising. This seems to be particularly true in the lives of young people.

This also explains why our country has experienced a dramatic rise in drug use and drug addiction. Philosopher John Gray is quite an interesting man. He is an atheist and has a very pessimistic view of life. In his book *Straw Dogs,* he confronts the question as to why drug addiction and drug abuse has proliferated so much. He says:

> "Drug use is a tacit admission of a forbidden truth in Western Culture. What is that truth? It is that for most people happiness is beyond reach."[38]

For most people, life is unavoidably hard and difficult, and they see no hope in their future. For those who live with an atheistic worldview, all happiness must be found in this lifetime and in this world. Yet, they are running up against this reality, and they cannot eliminate most of the sources of their unhappiness.

I would like to go back to Dr. Armand Nicholi, clinical professor of psychiatry at Harvard Medical School. In his book *The Question of God,* Nicholi contends that one of the major factors that causes depression is a person's worldview. He found that students who have a secular, godless worldview seem to struggle more with depression and do not respond very quickly to treatment. Their struggle is a result of their feelings of cosmic insignificance. For so many of them, life seems pointless.[39]

Nicholi did a good bit of research on what happened to students at Harvard when they converted to Christianity—and how they experienced a dramatic change in their view of life and the world.

> "Before their conversion experience, they referred often to an emptiness and despondency, sometimes calling it existential despair. This depressive mood was partly related to a gap they felt between their social conscience on the one hand and their personal morality—how they actually lived—on the other. They appeared to struggle with the passage of time, with aging and death, as paradoxical as this may seem in this age group. They spoke despairingly of feeling old, of having accomplished little in their lives, and, as students, living a parasitical existence. Yet, after their conversion, they spoke of experiencing a sense of forgiveness that apparently helped them become less intolerant of themselves, helped them bridge the gap between what they felt they were and what they thought they ought to be, and provided resources outside themselves

that made the future bridging of this gap less hopeless.

Although their spiritual experience did not free them from alterations in mood, they spoke of a 'sense of joy' not previously known and a marked decrease in the feeling of utter hopelessness and despair that they had struggled with previously.

Finally, they spoke of spiritual resources that give strength and renewed hope and that foster a more open, more tolerant, and more loving spirit toward others. They referred frequently to the theological concepts of redemption and forgiveness as being instrumental in reducing their self-hatred."[40]

In Nicholi's book there is also a chapter comparing and contrasting Lewis's and Freud's views on happiness. They clearly represent polar opposite thoughts on this issue. Freud believed in the pleasure principle, and that happiness is rooted in pleasure. Lewis believed that virtue and character, rooted in the love of God, was the key to happiness.

Many scholars today believe that our culture looks to pleasure as the source of happiness because we are living under the spell cast by Freud, as he clearly was the most influential psychiatrist of the 20th century. Interestingly, Freud not only made a direct correlation between happiness and pleasure, but also believed that people live in psychological dysfunction and are unhappy because social conventions limit our doing what we really find pleasure in. In essence, Freud believed that people are not happy because they are not free to pursue outwardly what they desire to do inwardly. He also contended these moral social conventions caused people to feel guilty when they are violated, which leads to further unhappiness. However, with the passage of time and after sober reflection, Freud realized the pleasure principle created a real dilemma.[41]

Freud eventually concluded that physical pleasure was temporary and fleeting, and therefore unhappiness was unavoidable. His view of life was dark, ominous, and full of despair. In a letter to his fiancé he admitted over a fourteen-month period that he had experienced only three or four days of happiness. Nicholi says that Freud constantly experienced 'feelings of hopelessness and helplessness, a negative interpretation of life with frequent thoughts of death, and a pessimistic view of the future.' The only thing he found that consistently lifted his spirits was a new drug called cocaine. At the end of his life he asked the question, 'What good to us is a long life if it is difficult and barren of joys, and if it is so full of misery that we can only welcome death as a deliverer?'[42]

For thirty-one years of his life, C.S. Lewis was also an atheist, and Nicholi says that during those years, Lewis shared Freud's despair. After becoming a Christian, he openly shared that his gloom was clearly a result of his godless worldview. He had concluded that the universe was a "menacing and unfriendly place." He saw no hope for the future.

However, everything changed when he became a Christian. His somber view of life was transformed into a joy and a real sense of freedom. He said that once he had become a Christian, he "began to know what life really is and what would have been lost by missing it."

In his book, Nicholi shares Lewis's ideas about true happiness:

> "Lewis asserts that the primary purpose of our lives—the reason for our existence on this planet—is to establish a relationship with the Person who placed us here. Until that relationship is established, all of our attempts to attain happiness—our quest for recognition, for money, for power, for the perfect marriage or the ideal friendship, for all that we spend our lives seeking—will always fall short, will never quite satisfy the longing, fill the void, quell the restlessness, or make us happy. Lewis explains that "God designed the human machine to run on Himself. He Himself is the fuel our spirits were designed to burn, or the food our spirits were designed to feed on...God cannot give us happiness and peace apart from Himself, because it is not there. There is no such thing."[43]

The Christian worldview sees pleasure as a gift from God; it brings delight into our lives. It is to be enjoyed within the boundaries God has given us. However, pleasure can never satisfy us, nor can it provide the deep-seated happiness that we all yearn for. God intended for our relationships with others and most significantly our relationship with Him to be the foundation of true happiness.

After studying the lives of Freud and Lewis, Nicholi concludes each of these men's worldview had a profound impact on their capacity to experience happiness.

6.

The Psychology of Unbelief

"The greatest aberration of the mind is to believe a thing to be, because we desire it."

—LOUIS PASTEUR

6.1

Psychological Reasons To Believe

OVER THE years, there has been a great deal discussed and written about the existence of God and why you should or should not believe in Him. Many different arguments have been made, and all types of evidence considered. But what about psychological reasons for believing in God or not believing in Him?

One of the first people to consider this was Sigmund Freud. In the early 1900s he came out with the thesis that religion, particularly Christianity, was simply the projection of a human's needs. It is the fulfillment of deep-seated wishes.

If belief in God is rooted in deep-seated wishes, then God is nothing more than an illusion. Freud writes in his book *Future of Illusions:*

> "We shall tell ourselves that it would be very nice if there were a God who created the world and was a benevolent providence and if there were a moral order in the universe and an afterlife, but it is a very striking fact that all this is exactly as we are bound to wish it to be."[1]

Freud saw the God of the Bible as merely a projection of powerful wishes and inner needs. He writes, "…religious ideas, which are given out as teachings…are illusions, fulfillments of the oldest, strongest and most urgent wishes of mankind." Freud admits that this theory originated with German philosopher Ludwig Feuerbach, but he was the one who was best known for promoting it.

So many people believe that faith in God is nothing more than a human invention that meets a human need.

Therefore, R.C. Sproul counters by asking why would those who invent God, particularly those who wrote the Bible, create a God who demands holiness from His people and whose holiness was more terrifying than the forces of nature? You would think they would instead create a more loving, docile, grandfatherly figure who was there to protect and comfort them.[2]

On the other hand, is it possible that God exists and it is the atheist who lives with the illusion and the false ideas? Could there be psychological reasons that cause people to disbelieve in God? This section will address this question and will provide several valid reasons why people do not want God in their lives and therefore choose to disbelieve in Him.

To gain some insight into the psychology of belief, consider C.S. Lewis. As a skeptic, he was quite surprised that his very intelligent friend J.R.R. Tolkien believed not only in God but Jesus as the Son of God. As Lewis began his spiritual search, he continued to gain new insights that were clearly in conflict with his current atheistic beliefs. He then became acutely aware of something that was happening to him. His intellect was taking him in a direction that his heart did not want to go. His mind was being drawn to that which he recognized to be true, but his heart was resistant. He later realized he was attracted to atheism because of the moral freedom it provided. He saw Jesus as someone who wanted to interfere with his life.

I read recently how Charles Darwin grew up believing in God, and that most people assume he rejected God when he developed his theory of natural selection. However, Darwin himself concedes that he lost his faith because of the Christian doctrine of hell. Others believe he also abandoned his belief in God when his ten-year-old daughter, Annie, passed away. Those close to him also sensed that Darwin was angry with God. Many people see disbelief as a way to get revenge toward Him.[3]

Finally, in the essays to follow, I will refer to the research of Dr. Paul Vitz a number of times. Vitz, a psychologist, earned his bachelor's degree at the University of Michigan and his PhD at Stanford University. He spent his career teaching at New York University. He was an atheist until his late 30s and today is considered an expert in the psychology of atheism.

Vitz says that atheists often develop their beliefs because of non-rational psychological reasons, not because of investigation of the evidence and coming to a sound rational conclusion. So, I think out of intellectual integrity every atheist should ask themselves, "How did I come to the conclusion that God does not exist? Did I truly investigate and examine the evidence, and then conclude there was no God?"

Vitz also says that the human heart is truly difficult to understand and fathom. It is hard to understand its deceptiveness. We need to better understand ourselves and our motives. In the essays in this section we will seek to understand the psychological barriers of believing in God.

6.2

A Reason Not To Believe

BACK IN 2004, I entered an essay into the John Templeton Foundation Power of Purpose essay contest. Since there were several thousand contestants, it was no surprise that my essay did not place or win an award. However, I did have the opportunity to read the winning essay by August Turak. It was a story of how a powerful encounter with a Trappist monk changed his life. One of the stories he tells reveals a great deal about what is at the heart of spiritual belief.

Turak describes a spiritual retreat he attended at an isolated monastery. He spent a great deal of time in solitude, but spent some time talking with someone whom they called a "spiritual director." His spiritual director was a man they knew as "Father Christian," who was 88 years old, spoke several languages, and had three PhDs.

"One afternoon in a one-on-one meeting with Father Christian, they got into a discussion on faith and belief. Father Christian launched into a story about a Presbyterian minister having a crisis of faith and leaving the ministry. The man was a friend of his, and Christian took his crisis so seriously that he actually left the monastery and traveled to his house in order to do what he could. The two men spent countless hours in fruitless theological debate. Finally dropping his voice, Christian looked the man steadily in the face and said, 'Bob, is everything in your life all right?' The minister said everything was fine. But the minister's wife called Christian a few days later. She had overheard Christian's question and her husband's answer, and she told Father Christian that the minister was having an affair and was leaving her as well as his ministry.

Christian fairly spat with disgust. He was wasting his time. Bob's problem was that he couldn't take the contradiction between his preaching and his living. So, God gets the boot. Remember this: All philosophical problems are, at the heart, moral problems. It all comes down to how you intend to live your life."[4]

One of the great philosophical thinkers of the 20th century was Mortimer Adler. He taught philosophy at the University of Chicago. He also helped found the Aspen Institute. Adler was co-editor of the 55-volume series entitled *The Great Books of the Western World* and was the sole author of 52 additional books.

For most of his life, he was a self-described pagan. Then, to the shock of his colleagues, he became a Christian at the age of 82. Adler lived to be 98 years old, and as he reflected back on his life, he acknowledged that at times he had been intrigued by the Christian faith. Even so, he never took the leap. As he examined his heart, Adler realized that he ultimately did not want to change his lifestyle. He did not want to live the Christian life; instead, he wanted to be free to live the way that he wanted. He said, "The decision to become a Christian lies in the state of one's heart (will), not in the state of one's mind." It dawned on Adler late in life that his atheism was not intellectually driven; it came down to how he wanted to live his life.[5]

When it gets right down to it, so many people are not on a truth and wisdom quest but rather on a search for pleasure and happiness. It comes very naturally to be guided by our feelings and emotions and not by reason and the yearning to live in harmony with what is true. In other words, our quest for pleasure and happiness takes priority over reason and sound decision-making that leads to our personal well-being.

I remember how shocked I was several years ago when I read where the well-known atheist Aldous Huxley gave his reason for being an atheist. In his book *Ends and Means*, he says:

> "I wanted to believe the Darwinian idea. I chose to believe it not because I think there was enormous evidence for it, nor because it had the full authority to give interpretation to my origins, but I chose to believe it because it delivered me from trying to find meaning and freed me to my own erotic passions."[6]

Think about what he is saying. This is a very intelligent man who says he does not believe in evolution because of the evidence. In fact, he is acknowledging there is not that much evidence for believing it. He did not want sexual restrictions, which God imposes upon us. For this reason, Huxley was drawn to atheism, in large part because it provided sexual liberation.

The great St. Augustine even acknowledged that he resisted God for a long period of time because of his desire for sexual pleasure. In his autobiography, he admits that intellectual arguments he made against believing in God was a smokescreen. He states very honestly, "The plain fact was, I thought I should be impossibly miserable without the embraces of a mistress."[7]

Modern people resist God because so much is at stake. We come up with all types of reasons not to believe in God, but cannot admit that our real problem is not a matter of the intellect but a matter of the heart and the will.

Dr. Scott Peck shares a true story that powerfully demonstrates the resistance of the heart. It is the story of one of his patients, Charlene. She struggled with depression and experienced a sense of meaninglessness in her life. As Peck asked questions and probed, he learned that she had apparently grown up in the church and had a belief in God. Peck described her as having a "well-developed, religious worldview." He asked why her beliefs did not make a difference in her life and help her with her sense of meaninglessness. There was a silence, and then she exploded with this incredible admission:

> "I cannot do it. There is no room for me in that. That would be my death. I don't want to live for God. I will not. I want to live for me. For my own sake."[8]

What an incredibly honest admission. This woman's response is a picture of the human heart resisting God, refusing to surrender to God. And she gives the reason: "I want to live my life for me."

This is the heart of the human condition. If God is real, and the Christian worldview is true, then it is only logical for us to live under His authority and adopt the Christian worldview. Yet so many resist the authority of God. They desire to be autonomous and to be a law unto themselves. They do not want to give up control of their lives. I have encountered many people who find it much easier to proclaim that God does not exist than to acknowledge His existence and intentionally choose to reject Him.

6.3
Willful Blindness

WHEN PEOPLE establish a belief, they should do so because they are utterly convinced that what they are believing, that which they are putting their confidence in, is true.

Truth is paramount. The idea of truth has always been very straightforward. Truth is that which is ultimately, finally, and absolutely real. Truth is the "way it is" and therefore is utterly trustworthy and dependable. Accuracy is an essential component of truth. In fact, truth does not yield to opinion, popular fashion, or even a person's sincerity of belief. It does not matter how sincerely you believe something if, in the end, it is false. Truth is in harmony with reality, and we should therefore always seek to live our lives in harmony with what is true.

As human beings, we have, however, an unusual relationship with the truth. There is a side of us that wants to pursue the truth, particularly if it is leading us in a direction we want to go. On the other hand, we seem to balk when it leads us in a direction we do not want to go.

Often, we establish beliefs because they generally express how we want life to be. This is why Blaise Pascal says, "People almost invariably arrive at their beliefs not on the basis of proof but on the basis of what they find attractive."

This reminds me of the documentary *Enron, The Smartest Guys in the Room.* In the documentary, they reveal that Jeffrey

Skilling, the leader of Enron, had his eyesight corrected via LASIK surgery. After this, it seems that all employees who wore glasses followed his lead, so that no one wore glasses. The creator of the documentary saw this as a metaphor for what was going on in the company. No one was looking closely, for the longest time, at how Enron was producing such immense profitability. As journalist Joe Morgenstern described it, "For those inside Enron, as well as those outside looking in, this epic corporate scandal was a case of willful blindness."[9]

Willful blindness is a term used in the legal profession. It refers to any situation in which people intentionally turn their attention away from an ethical problem because the problem is too disturbing to deal with. We are afraid to look reality in the eye, because it may take us in a direction we don't want to go. C.S. Lewis believed this was one of the great flaws in our character. In psychology it is called denial or suppression, where we suppress thoughts or beliefs that are painful or disturbing.

This reminds me of an old classic movie that I watched several years ago. It was titled *Judgment at Nuremberg*, and was based on the true story of the Nuremberg trials where a number of Nazi leaders, who survived the war, are accused of crimes against humanity for their involvement in the atrocities committed under the Nazi regime. During one trial, they seek to discover how the German people could so easily turn blind eyes and deaf ears to the crimes of the Nazi regime.

I remember the actor Burt Lancaster being questioned on the witness stand in his role as a German war criminal. The prosecutor, in questioning Lancaster, wanted to know how the German people could not have known what was happening to the Jews. He responded, "If the German people said they did not know, it was because they did not want to know." The thought of their beloved country being involved in mass exterminations was intolerable. Instead of accepting the hard truth and attempting to stop the Nazi atrocities, many of the German people simply chose to deny the reality of the Holocaust altogether. This is clearly a picture of willful blindness.

This seems to be part of the human condition. Several years ago, there was an interesting interview in *Fortune* magazine with Warren Buffet. He spoke of his philosophy on purchasing stocks. He then spoke of a flaw we human beings have in our makeup. He said that we all seem to have within us a psychological force that causes us to cling to our ideas and beliefs, even in the face of contradictory information. He then said to an interviewer:

> "Now, there was a smart man who did just about the hardest thing in the world to do. Charles Darwin used to say that whenever he ran into something that contradicts a conclusion he cherished, he was obliged to write on paper the finding within 30 minutes. Otherwise, his mind would work to reject the discordant information, much as the body rejects transplants."[10]

Ultimately, Buffet was saying that in order to live wisely, you have to love and be committed to what is true. However, the problem is that we would rather cling to our old beliefs, even if they are false.

There is an event in the New Testament where you see a very clear incidence of willful blindness. Jesus has just performed a stunning miracle, by raising Lazarus from the dead. Lazarus had been in the tomb for four days, and Jesus had the stone moved from the entrance and then ordered Lazarus to come forth. There were a number of witnesses present who obviously were stunned when this dead man of four days walked out.

What is interesting is that many of those witnessing the event went straight to the Jewish religious leaders to report what had happened. These leaders had been hearing rumors that Jesus might be their long-awaited Messiah. You would think that after learning of this incredible miracle, they might wonder if Jesus was, in fact, the Messiah. You would think they might want to question Him to see if he was the one they had been waiting for over the centuries. Instead, these religious leaders realized that if Jesus continued these astonishing miracles, they would lose all of their followers and the Romans would take away their power. Instead of pursuing the truth, they began to plot how to get rid of Jesus. This is another clear example of willful blindness. They clung to their position of power and prestige instead of pursuing the truth concerning the Jewish Messiah, which was at the heart of their religious tradition.

We must recognize and come to an understanding of this natural tendency that exists in each of us. Unchecked fear always leads to denial, and we may find that we consciously deny truth its rightful place in our lives because we fear the results it may bring. This is especially true when it comes to God and spiritual reality.

6.4

Willful Blindness in the Sciences

IN MY research, I have found that willful blindness is quite common among atheists, particularly in the world of science.

One of the most prominent astronomers in the last century was Dr. Robert Jastrow. He received his PhD from Columbia University and then worked for a number of years at NASA, until taking a position at Dartmouth, where he taught for 11 years.

Jastrow was agnostic, but spoke of willful blindness in his book, *God and the Astronomers.* He described how scientists react when they encounter evidence they do not like. He says:

> "Their reactions provide an interesting demonstration of the response of the scientific mind—supposedly a very objective mind—when evidence uncovered by science itself leads to a conflict with the articles of faith in our professions. It turns out that the scientist behaves the way the rest of us do when our beliefs are in conflict with the evidence. We become irritated, we pretend the conflict does not exist, or we paper it over with meaningless phrases."[11]

This is what so often happens in our lives when we encounter evidence that contradicts a long-held belief—we pretend the conflict does not exist. We become willfully blind and, in the process, become irresponsible in what we believe.

In his book *The Creator and the Cosmos,* astrophysicist Hugh Ross shares an interesting event in the life of Albert Einstein.

> "It was 1916 and Albert Einstein didn't like where his calculations were leading him. If his theory of General Relativity was true, it meant that the universe was not eternal but had a beginning. Einstein's calculations indeed were revealing a definite beginning to all time, all matter, and all space. This flew in the face of his belief that the universe was static and eternal.
>
> Einstein later called his discovery "irritating." He wanted the universe to be self-existent—not reliant on any outside cause—but the universe appeared to be one giant effect. In fact, Einstein so disliked the implications of General Relativity—a theory that is now proven accurate to five decimal places—that he introduced a cosmological constant (which some have called a "fudge factor") into his equations in order to show that the universe is static and to avoid an absolute beginning."[12]

Clearly, Einstein did not like the direction the evidence was taking him. To believe that the universe had a beginning, that it was finite, and therefore there was some type of cause behind it all would disrupt his life as a scientist. For this reason, he came up with a fudge factor. However, according to Ross this fudge factor did not last long.

> "In 1919, British cosmologist Arthur Eddington conducted an experiment during a solar eclipse which confirmed that General Relativity was indeed true—the universe wasn't static but had a beginning. Like Einstein, Eddington wasn't happy with the implications. He later wrote, 'Philosophically, the notion of a beginning of the present order of nature is repugnant to me . . . I should like to find a genuine loophole.'
>
> By 1922, Russian mathematician Alexander Friedmann had officially exposed Einstein's fudge factor as an algebraic

> error. (Incredibly, in his quest to avoid a beginning, the great Einstein had divided by zero—something even schoolchildren know is a no-no!) Meanwhile, Dutch astronomer Willem de Sitter had found that General Relativity required the universe to be expanding. And in 1927, the expanding of the universe was actually observed by astronomer Edwin Hubble (namesake of the space telescope).
>
> Looking through the 100-inch Hooker telescope at California's Mount Wilson Observatory, Hubble discovered a "red shift" in the light from every observable galaxy, which meant that those galaxies were moving away from us. In other words, General Relativity was again confirmed—the universe appears to be expanding from a single point in the distant past.
>
> In 1929, Einstein made a pilgrimage to Mount Wilson to look through Hubble's telescope for himself. What he saw was irrefutable. The observational evidence showed that the universe was indeed expanding as General Relativity had predicted. With his cosmological constant now completely crushed by the weight of the evidence against it, Einstein could no longer support his wish for an eternal universe. He subsequently described the cosmological constant as 'the greatest blunder of my life,' and he redirected his efforts to find the box top to the puzzle of life. Einstein said that he wanted 'to know how God created the world. I am not interested in this or that phenomenon, in the spectrum of this or that element. I want to know His thoughts; the rest are details.'"[13]

Do you see what Einstein had been doing? Initially, he was allowing his beliefs to shape the evidence in his research. Eventually, he realized that he must be honest and allow the evidence to shape his theories. Therefore, he changed his belief about the beginning of the universe and in the process discovered the theory of relativity.

This is why, later in life, Einstein made a very important observation about science. He said, "Most people think it is the intellect which makes a great scientist. They are wrong. It is their character." Einstein recognized that the key to being a great scientist is to follow the evidence and the truth, wherever it leads you.

One of the most influential books of science in the last century was Thomas Kuhn's *The Structure of Scientific Revolutions.* It was about the progress of scientific knowledge. Kuhn was a superb historian who focused on the great advances of science through which he called "revolutions," which are so often hindered by holding on to old beliefs.

I think it is so easy to believe that scientists are immune to the influence of their own beliefs and biases as they do research. We have this presumption that scientists are dispassionate and unbiased individuals who are committed to the truth and always simply report the facts.

Kuhn's book points out this fallacy, as his research into the history of science reveals that scientists are clearly not objective. He provides dozens of historical cases that prove researchers are far from being neutral and unbiased, particularly in testing and evaluating results. He makes it clear that scientists have a real tendency to hold on tenaciously to their theories, even though they face contradicting data.[14]

The late Dr. Herbert Schlossberg, a leading historian and scholar, made this observation:

> "Thomas Kuhn concluded that at a given time any scientific community will always have in its structure an element that is more will than intellect, a product of personal history."[15]

It is the same idea that we explored in the prior essay "Psychological Reasons To Believe" (6.1), referencing the spiritual journey of C.S. Lewis:

> "...his intellect was taking him in a direction his heart did not want to go."

Back in August of 2014, David Brooks wrote an article in *The New York Times* titled "The Mental Virtues." He refers to the book *Intellectual Virtues* by Robert Roberts and Jay Wood. In their book, they speak of the importance of having intellectual courage—the willingness to hold unpopular views. In the article, Brooks then makes reference to Kuhn:

> "Thomas Kuhn pointed out that scientists often simply ignore facts that don't fit their existing paradigms, but an intellectually courageous person is willing to look at things that are surprisingly hard to look at."[16]

C.S. Lewis wrote an essay titled "Modern Man and His Categories of Thought." Lewis remarks on how irrational people were becoming in their approach to their beliefs. In the audience where he was lecturing, he began to notice, "it is almost impossible to make them understand that I recommend Christianity because I think it is objectively true. But people today are simply not interested whether a religion is true or false..." Ultimately, he says, they are more interested in how it will impact their lives and their lifestyles.

6.5

The Problem of Pride

I REMEMBER meeting with a man in his early 20s who was clearly on a search for spiritual truth. In our first meeting, he informed me, "I am not sure I believe in God." We spent a good hour discussing the issue of God, and I shared with him my reasons for believing and then discussed his objections. I did not change his mind and assumed that there was no need to meet again. However, he wanted to continue and learn more about Christianity. So, we met three or four more times, and in our last meeting, he made an interesting confession: "I do believe in God, and I believe what you have told me is true. However, I am going to pass. Being a Christian might negatively impact my social life and my career."

When all was said and done, he was worried about how being a Christian would affect people's opinion of him. It also struck me it was easier for him to say, "I am not sure I believe in God," instead of admitting "I believe in Him, but I reject him."

The fear of rejection is a powerful force in our lives. We never seem to be able to shake it. I sometimes wonder if we realize how we gear our lives to meet the expectations and approval of others, particularly when it comes to our faith.

Psychotherapist Anthony de Mello makes this observation:

> "Look at your life and see how you have filled its emptiness with people. As a result, they have a stranglehold on you. See how they control your behavior by their approval and disapproval. They hold the power to ease your loneliness with their company, to send your spirits soaring with their praise, to bring you down to the depths with their criticism and rejection. Take a look at yourself spending almost every waking moment of your day placating and pleasing people, whether they are living or dead. You live by their norms, conform to their standards, seek their company, desire their love, dread their ridicule, long for their applause, meekly submit to the guilt they lay upon you; you are terrified to go against the fashion in the way you dress or speak or act or even think."[17]

I would like to come back to the psychologist Paul Vitz. As I mentioned in the first essay in this section, he was an atheist well into his 30s. His spiritual journey is quite interesting:

> "The major reason for me wanting to become an atheist was that I desired to be accepted by the powerful and influential psychologists in my field. In particular, I wanted to be accepted by my professors in graduate school. As a graduate student I was thoroughly socialized by the specific culture of academic psychology. My professors at Stanford, as much as they might disagree on psychological theory, were, as far as I could tell, united on really only two things: their intense personal ambitions and their rejection of religion. In this environment, just as I had learned how to dress like a college student by putting on the right clothes, I also learned to think like a proper psychologist by putting on the right, atheistic, skeptical ideas and attitudes."[18]

Vitz is essentially saying that he wanted to be accepted by his peers and professors. He feared their rejection, so he adopted their views, whether or not he believed them to be true.

Lee Strobel was an attorney with a law degree from Yale Law School and, for a number of years, was head of the legal affairs department at the *Chicago Tribune.* In his book *The Case for Faith,* he shares a conversation that he had with scholar and prolific author Dr. Lynn Anderson. Strobel and Anderson got into a conversation on the psychology of atheism. Anderson believes many atheists have certain underlying reasons for their unbelief that are not necessarily intellectual. Strobel asks him to give an example. Anderson responded:

> "When I was a youngster, a brilliant novelist—an atheist from an atheistic, communist family came to our little town in Canada to gather local color for a book he was writing. One day he was visiting with our family and he got real serious. He said, 'Can I ask you questions about your religion?' Even though I had been wrestling with doubts from time to time, I said yes.
>
> He asked, 'Do you really believe there's a God who knows my name?' I said, 'Yeah. That's what I believe.' He said, 'Do you believe the Bible's true? Babies born from virgins, dead people coming out of the cemetery?' I said, 'Yes, that's what I believe.'"

Then he said with great emotion:

> "'I'd give anything to believe that because I've traveled all over the world and I've seen that most people are miserable. The only people who really seem to be getting out of life what they want are the people who say they believe what you believe. But I just can't believe because my head keeps getting in the way!'
>
> Anderson's eyes got wide. 'I was blown away, Lee. I didn't know what to say next because his head was a lot smarter than mine!'
>
> Then Anderson leaned closer to me. 'But, in retrospect, I don't think his head was the real problem,' he said. 'I started thinking about what he would lose if he followed Jesus. He

> was part of a guild of brilliant writers who all think religion is a total crock. I really believc his professional pride and the rejection of his peers would have been too high of a price for him to pay.'"[19]

Journalist David Brooks of *The New York Times* believes one of the greatest truths he learned from his professors at the University of Chicago was to have intellectual courage. He says, "The hard part of intellectual life is separating what is true from what will get you liked."[20]

If you will recall in my essay on willful blindness, I describe how people responded to the news of Lazarus being raised from the dead by Jesus. I examined those whose personal ambitions were more important than the truth of God.

There was also a second response by those who had witnessed the resurrection of Lazarus. As Jesus was performing signs and miracles, many people, even some of the leading citizens, wanted to believe in Him. However, for fear of expulsion from the synagogue, they did not believe. John then makes this assessment: "For they loved the approval of men rather than the approval of God." (John 12:43)

It is amazing that we would allow the approval of men to set the boundaries of our faith. It has made me wonder how many of us have chosen a path of life not because it is the best and wisest path but because it meets the approval of the people in our sphere of influence, and the people we want to impress.

I do not think we are aware that there is one question we are always asking ourselves. It often seems to be the central question that must finally be answered before we make certain decisions, particularly on the issue of faith. It is a question that haunts the lives of many: *What will people think of me?* This question can impact us emotionally, psychologically, and spiritually.

However, when it comes to our decisions about God and spiritual truth, we need to realize how much is at stake. We all need to recognize that we are utter fools if we allow the approval of others to keep us from embracing God's eternal truth.

6.6

The Defective Father Theory

WHEN IT comes to psychological belief and atheism, one of the most fascinating theories I have encountered comes from a book by Paul Vitz, *Faith of the Fatherless. The Psychology of Atheism.* Vitz calls it the theory of the defective father. Ironically, one of the first people to articulate the theory was Freud himself. He stated it this way:

> "Psychoanalysis, which has taught us the intimate connection between the father complex and belief in God, has shown us that the personal God is logically nothing but an exalted father and daily demonstrates to us how youthful persons lose their religious belief as soon as the authority of their father breaks down."[21]

In other words, Freud was saying that once a child is disappointed with his or her father, or loses respect for the father, it is most difficult to believe in a heavenly father. This is also true if they lose the father to death, divorce, or any other reason the father might abandon the family. A small child sees it as their father has chosen to go away and abandon them. This is why Vitz calls it "the defective father theory."

The first two to investigate this theory were Dr. Lee Kirkpatrick and Dr. Phillip Shaver, both psychologists. Kirkpatrick, who is agnostic, cited an interesting study where 350 members of the American Association for the Advancement of Atheism were interviewed, with the intent of understanding the possible causes and reasons for their atheistic belief. What I find to be most fascinating is that 320 of the respondents, more than 90%, were men. Of these 320 men, almost all of them report having lost a parent during childhood or had poor relations with one or both parents. It should also be noted that these 350 atheists reported very much higher rates of unhappy childhood and unhappy adolescence than those who believe in God.[22]

Vitz concluded from this study that:

> "Whatever might weaken or harm the relationship of a child with his father or parents will, in general, predispose the child in adulthood to atheism or unbelief or to spiritualist beliefs without a personal God."[23]

Ten years before Vitz wrote the book, he was not even aware of the "defective father theory." He was doing some research on the lives of famous atheists, and, over time, he began to notice the bad relationships they had with their fathers. Dr. Vitz then decided to do a study of the most influential atheists in history, most particularly those who were what is called intense atheists. He studied those who were great thinkers—most of them were philosophers—and their rejection of God was central to their intellectual life. They are the people who are generally considered as the founders and promoters of modern atheism.

Friedrich Nietzsche, David Hume, Bertrand Russell, Jean-Paul Sartre, Albert Camus, and Arthur Schopenhauer all lost their fathers to death either before they were born or early in life. Nietzsche, for instance, had a very good relationship with his father, yet his father died when he was five. It was a great loss, which he never forgot. Nietzsche wrote that his father "died all too soon. I missed the strict and superior guidance of a male intellect." Furthermore, he saw nothing but a weakness and sickliness in his father's life during those years as a young boy, and he associated that with his father's Christian belief. Nietzsche always believed that Christianity was for weak people and that the Christian God suffered from an absence of "life force."

Vitz's research determined that Thomas Hobbes, Hans Meissner, Voltaire, Samuel Butler, Sigmund Freud, H.G. Wells, and Ludwig Feuerbach all had weak or abusive fathers. None of them had healthy relationships with their father.[24]

Then you have some of the New Atheists: Richard Dawkins, Daniel Dennett, and Christopher Hitchens. Dawkins spent a good part of his early life away from his father because he was sent off to boarding school. When he was nine years old and attending this strongly Anglican boarding school, he was sexually abused by the Latin master who was associated with the church. Vitz contends, and I would agree, that this experience created a strong negative association with Christianity.

Daniel Dennett's father died when he was five years old in a plane crash.

Christopher Hitchens's father was a very quiet man who rarely spoke to his son. Like Richard Dawkins, Christopher was away at boarding school from the age of eight to eighteen. Hitchens says he has very few memories of his father during those years. On the other hand, he was very close to his mother. However, when he was in college, she left her husband and eloped with a former Anglican priest. Not long after that, his mother and her new husband made a suicide pact and killed themselves. Hitchens was devastated by this and clearly saw this Anglican clergyman as the essential cause of his mother's suicide.[25]

Vitz also examines the lives of political leaders who were atheists and hated religion.

Joseph Stalin's father was a very rough and violent man. He drank heavily and often would beat Joseph's mother violently. One of Stalin's best friends growing up made this observation: "Undeserved and severe beatings made the boy as hard and heartless as his father was." As a political leader, he persecuted the Orthodox church in Russia with great vigor, murdering thousands of Orthodox priests.

Adolf Hitler's father also gave his son regular, severe beatings. He was described as being authoritarian, hard, unsympathetic, and short tempered. Adolf seemed to be the child that caught the brunt of his father's rage. When Hitler turned fourteen his father died, and from that point on, he never had a male father figure to lead and guide him. Those who have studied his life believe that from this point forward the teaching of Nietzsche had a profound influence on his life, and is what led to many of his radical ideas of building a master race.[26]

Vitz did find several men who were atheists who could be considered exceptions to his theory. Dennis Diderot was one of the major figures of the French Enlightenment. He and his father seemed to have a positive relationship up until the time he was a young man. Diderot wanted to marry a woman that his father disapproved of, and so his father kidnapped his son to prevent the marriage. He eventually escaped and married the woman. It was around this period that Diderot came out with his outspoken belief in atheism, which became a source of estrangement between him and his strong Catholic family. From this point on, he and his father were never reconciled.

Karl Marx, the father of Marxism and Communism, was a very prominent atheist, though he did not spend much time promoting the atheistic worldview. Marx's relationship with his father seemed to not have much conflict, but the young Marx did not seem to have much respect for his father. He watched the elder Marx convert to Protestant Christianity primarily for social reasons. And as young Marx developed his own theories as a teen, he suddenly and radically rejected the family's wealthy background. Vitz says, "His lifetime commitment to communist theory can be said to be a long-term, violent attack on everything his father represented."[27]

Two years ago, I was speaking to a gentleman who had helped me on a couple of book projects. When we finished talking, he asked if I would pray for his two grandsons, who had become atheists. I had just learned of Vitz's defective father theory, and so I asked him about his grandsons' relationship with their father. He responded, "They hate his guts."

I realize the defective father theory is just a theory, but it seems to be validated by some very good research. It has to cause you to wonder what kind of difference it would have made if each of these men had experienced the influence of a loving proactive father. It also has to cause you to wonder how many atheists in the world have adopted their belief because of non-rational psychological factors, and not from the evidence for the existence of God.

7.

The Battle with Science

"I think that science without religion is lame and, conversely, religion without science is blind."

—ALBERT EINSTEIN

7.1

Science and Faith

THIS FIRST essay will serve as an introduction to the issue of science and the belief in God.

There seems to be three ways people view the relationship between science and God.

The first is this: Science and religious belief are at war with each other. That's the approach Richard Dawkins and the New Atheists have taken. And most people who share this view also believe that science has the overwhelming edge in credibility because it's all about provable facts and religion depends on faith.

The second view is that science and religious beliefs have nothing to do with each other. In other words, they are two separate and distinct realms that don't intersect or interact at all. Stephen J. Gould taught at Harvard and was considered one of the world's prominent paleontologists. He was an outspoken atheist.

But Gould was very clear that it wasn't his science that brought him to that position. He argues in his very interesting book *Rock of Ages* that science simply cannot, by the legitimate application of its method, comment on the God question. In other words, it simply lies beyond the scientific method. Gould believed that science and faith occupy distinct different domains. Science covers the empirical universe, while religion extends to the issue of morality, values, and meaning.

Finally, the third way to view the relationship is that the testimony of science points to—it doesn't prove—the existence of God. There are a large number of credentialed and highly respected professors, in all scientific disciplines—such as astrophysics, biology, medicine, sociology, archeology, chemistry, cosmology—who believe there is a very strong case for theism at the heart of the universe.

Dr. Stephen Meyer, who has degrees in physics, geology, and a doctorate in history and philosophy of science, all from the prestigious Cambridge University, says:

> "In fact, across a wide range of scientists, evidence has come to light in the last 50 years which, taken together, provide a robust case for theism."[1]

I believe Dr. Francis Collins has given us balanced perspective on science and faith.

> "Science really is only legitimately able to comment on things that are part of nature. And science is really good at that, but if you're going to try to take the tools of science and disprove God, you're in the wrong territory. Science has to remain silent on the question of anything that falls outside of the natural world."[2]

But does the latest science seem to point to the existence of God? Could it be that science is itself evolving in the face of new discoveries, new evidence, and bold critical thinking? Can we detect a revived openness in the scientific community to the possibility of an ultimate creator? What are the facts? According to a survey of the members of the American Association for the Advancement of Science conducted by the Pew Research Center in May and June of 2009, 51% of scientists said they believed in God or a higher power, while 41% said they did not.[3]

Think about the significance of this. If scientific evidence was conclusive and could prove that God does not exist, then all scientists would be atheists. Therefore, it is clear that science can neither prove nor disprove the existence of God. However, as you will see in these next essays, science can be a signpost that points to the reality of God. If you will recall what the notorious atheist Antony Flew had to say about the reason he changed his mind:

> "The short answer is this—this is the world picture as I see it that has emerged from modern science."

One final thought about science that is pertinent to this issue is our need to understand that in modern science there are two broad categories that are operating. The first is operational science and involves testing, observing, and measuring and leads to technological progress. We have seen operational science have an impact on our computers, satellites, mobile phones, medicines, and medical procedures. This enables us to increase our understanding of how our world works and how to improve our lives and our standard of living.

The second category, ongoing science is about studying the world and seeking to understand the past. So, when you use the word "science" you need to know these two functions of science are very different and cannot be regarded in the same way. However, there is a great deal of confusion in popular science over these two areas of investigation. You cannot give them the same weight.[4]

For instance, when we send people into space, there is a great deal of certainty that the rockets will function properly because they have been rigorously tested. They are reliable. However, when you consider the issues we will be looking at in the essays in this section, you will recognize they are not testable. It is more of a forensic nature in that you study evidence in an attempt to understand the past. You will see in the essays to come that theories developed in the ongoing sciences over time can be proven to be false.

For instance, philosopher and theologian Dr. Joe Boot says:

> "So when the BBC screens "Walking with Dinosaurs" and talks as though it is a known fact that the Earth is billions of years old, during which time life spontaneously evolved from a primordial soup, we assume that these assertions must work equally well scientifically—but they do not! As these assumptions are so frequently heard, they appear authoritative. Add to that the deep voice of the narrator and the impressive computer graphics, and we are convinced. Yet, the evidence for these claims is often weak and unclear."[5]

In fact, as you will see, the theory that life began on this planet from a primordial pool of chemicals that was struck by lightning has been proven to be absolutely false, though for many years it was believed and taught to be a known fact.

7.2

A Ground-Shaking Discovery

FOR MUCH of the last century, cosmologists believed the universe was eternal, that it always existed. For this reason, no one needed to know the origin of the universe because it did not have a beginning. This belief supported an atheistic worldview.

However, with the commencement of a new century there were a number of breakthroughs in the field of physics and astronomy. Einstein discovered the theory of relativity, which helped us understand how the world works. Most historians agree, however, the most ground-shaking discovery came from the astronomer Edwin Hubble. In 1929, he observed through his telescope a phenomenon that would change the world. He was able to see that the light measured from various stars appeared to be red. What this means if the light of a star is redder, it is moving away from the Earth. This red-shift effect meant that all distant galaxies are moving away from the Earth. In other words, the universe was expanding. Therefore, if you took this expanding universe and reversed this expansion, it would all come back to a single starting point. This discovery came to be called "The Big Bang Theory." This theory postulates that the universe had a beginning; it had to have had a cause. This did not sit well with astronomers who were atheists because "The Big Bang Theory" points to God. Some kind of supreme being had to be the cause.[6]

Astronomer Robert Jastrow, an agnostic who was the former head of the Goddard Institute for Space Studies at NASA, had this to say upon the learning of "The Big Bang Theory."

> "When a scientist writes about God, his colleagues assume he is either over the hill or going bonkers. In my case it should be understood from the start that I am agnostic in religious matters...However, I am fascinated by the implications in some of the scientific developments of recent years. The essence of these developments is that the universe had, in some sense, a beginning—that it began at a certain moment in time."[7]

So many astronomers downplayed this new discovery because of its religious implications. Sir Arthur Eddington was an English astronomer and physicist. Listen to his words of reluctance in accepting the Big Bang:

> "Philosophically, the notion of a beginning of the present order of Nature is repugnant to me . . . I should like to find a genuine loophole."[8]

Later, he reached a point where he felt he had no choice but to believe it. He said,

> "The beginning seems to present insuperable difficulties unless we agree to look on it as frankly supernatural."[9]

The predominant view in cosmology today is The Big Bang Theory, which states that the universe is expanding from a single point in the distant past. In other words, at some definite point in the dimension of time there was a uniquely massive explosion, what scientists call a "singularity," and the universe has been expanding ever since. Thus, since the universe had an actual beginning, then, arguably, The Big Bang Theory points rather conspicuously to a theistic view of the universe.

The Big Bang is profoundly theistic.

In fact, I read recently that it is hard to find a cosmologist that will want to participate in a public debate on the existence of God. What's happened in their branch of science makes the atheistic point of view extremely difficult to defend.

Dr. Allan Sandage is widely considered the greatest observational cosmologist in the world. He has been awarded all types of honors, including astronomy's equivalent of the Nobel Prize. In the 1980s he stunned the scientific world when he announced that he had become a Christian. He disclosed this at a conference he was attending and said the Big Bang is clearly a supernatural event that cannot be explained within the realm of physics. He said:

> "It was my science that drove me to this conclusion…It was only through the supernatural that I can understand the mystery of existence…"[10]

And returning to Stephen Meyer from Cambridge, he said this:

> "You can invoke neither time nor space nor matter nor energy nor the laws of nature to explain the origin of the universe. General relativity points to the need for a cause that transcends those domains. And theism affirms the existence of such an entity, namely God. In short, naturalism is on hard times in cosmology; the deeper you get into it, the harder it is to get rid of the God hypothesis."[11]

As Nobel Prize winner Arno Penzias said about the Big Bang:

> "The best data we have are exactly what I would have predicted had I nothing to go on but the first five books of Moses, the Psalms, and the Bible as a whole."[12]

Finally, the prominent world-renowned British theoretical physicist Stephen Hawking said this:

> "Almost everyone now believes that the universe and time itself had a beginning at the Big Bang."[13]

Hawking goes on to say:

> "The odds against a universe like ours emerging out of something like the Big Bang are enormous. I think there are clearly religious implications." Elsewhere he says, "It would be very difficult to explain why the universe would have begun in just this way except as the act of a God who intended to create beings like us."[14]

Finally, he admits that:

> "Many people do not like the idea that time has a beginning, probably because it smacks of divine intervention."[15]

These are stunning words from the world's most prominent scientist since Einstein.

Serious and curious thinkers recognize this is one of the big questions of life. How did the universe begin? How did something come from nothing? Science has clearly concluded that the universe is not eternal and is not a result of an uncaused source. The atheistic worldview does not have a credible response to the origin of the universe.

Taken together, The Big Bang Theory and Einstein's theory of relativity each provide a scientific description of what Christians call "creatio ex nihilo," a Latin phrase that translates to "creation out of nothing." It comes from Paul's words from Romans that God "calls into being that which does not exist." Maybe this explains the beginning of the universe. Maybe Paul had it right?

7.3
The Beginning of Life

Another major question has to do with the origin of life on planet Earth. This world is clearly suitable for plant, animal, and human life, but how did it begin? How did life arise from nothing?

Up until the 1970s, maybe even the 1980s, the prevailing belief in science stemming from Darwin's landmark work was that if you were to go back to the primeval beginnings of the Earth, you would find it covered with countless pools of water amid barren and rocky expanses, chemically enriched with the "necessary ingredients" to create life. These small bodies of water and their ingredients are referred to as "primordial soup," and, as the theory goes, the Earth at that time was an intense environment of constant electrical activity. Lightning would, of course, regularly strike this soup, at which point various amino acids, the building blocks of life, would be formed. Once these amino acids were formed, natural selection somehow takes over and life begins to evolve. Millions of years later, here we are, building computers and flying all over the world in airplanes. This theory really took off in 1953 when a scientist named Stanley Miller demonstrated, in the laboratory, how this could actually happen.

Miller created a pool of chemicals, the "necessary ingredients" to create an amino acid. He then pumped electrical charges into it, and amino acids were formed. As you can imagine, Darwinian scientists were elated because if the origin of life can be explained solely through natural processes, then God is no longer necessary.[16]

Lee Strobel said that when he heard this taught in his high school biology class, it dramatically transformed his belief in God and led him to atheism. He said, "That's when I became an atheist." I, too, remember being taught this in my high school biology class.

Miller's experiment was hailed as a major breakthrough in science. Carl Sagan believed it was one of the most significant things that happened in man's quest for knowledge because it proved that life could arise on other planets.

The only way for Miller's experiment to work, however, is that the atmosphere of the Earth had to be a hydrogen-rich mixture of methane, ammonia, and water vapor. The only problem with this theory is that there is no real evidence for such an atmosphere. Still there were those who believed the theory was sound because the experiment did produce amino acids.[17]

Then in the 1980s, NASA scientists actually demonstrated that the primitive Earth had little if any volume of methane, ammonia, or hydrogen. Instead, the atmosphere at that time was composed of water, carbon dioxide, and nitrogen. This new information blew Miller's theory right out of the water. Miller's experiment, a theory on the origins of life, which had been taught for years as an indisputable scientific fact, imploded. And twenty-first century science doesn't, in fact, have any indisputable evidence on how life began on Earth. Miller admitted the following in the periodical *Scientific American* nearly forty years after his famous experiment:

> "The problem of the origin of life has turned out to be much more difficult than I, and most other people, envisioned."[18]

Klaus Dose, a biochemist who is considered by the National Academy of Sciences as being at the highest level of expertise on the origin of life, says:

> "More than thirty years of experimentation on the origin of life in the fields of chemical and molecular evolution have led to a better perception of the immensity of the problem of the origin of life on Earth rather than to its solution. At present, all discussions on principal theories and experiments in the field either end in stalemate or in a confession of ignorance."[19]

In fact, Nobel Prize-winning scientist Francis Crick, who, along with James Watson and Maurice Wilkins, discovered the molecular structure of DNA, says:

> "Every time I write a paper on the origin of life, I swear I will never write another one because there is too much speculation running after too few facts."[20]

Then Crick continues—and bear in mind, he was antagonistic toward any belief in God whatsoever:

> "The origin of life appears to be almost a miracle… So many are the conditions which would have to be satisfied to get it going."[21]

Allan Sandage, whom we discussed earlier, who was honored in the astronomical field for having established the most reasonable and accurate estimation for the Hubble constant and the age of the universe and for which he won the National Medal of Science, concluded that God is,

> "…the explanation for the miracle of existence."[22]

Even Charles Darwin acknowledged:

> "Science as yet throws no light on the far higher problems of the essence or origin of life."[23]

Dr. John Lennox is an Emeritus Professor of Mathematics at the University of Oxford, and an Emeritus Fellow in Mathematics and Philosophy of Science as well as a Pastoral Advisor at Green Templeton College, Oxford. An author and popular lecturer on the interface between science, philosophy, and theology, he has participated in a number of debates with atheists Richard Dawkins and Christopher Hitchens.

Lennox relates a fascinating story about a brilliant scientist in England, a man by the name of Andrew Parker, who is the director of research at the Natural History Museum in London. He holds professorships in a Chinese university as well as an Australian university. Lennox said he has known him for a number of years and that he is an expert in "bioluminescence," a field that studies the production and emission of light by living organisms. Specifically, Parker studies marine life that emits light, and, in his research, he came to the conclusion that the eye has played a central role in evolutionary biology.

One day Parker was giving a lecture on the subject of bioluminescence and a reporter in the back of the room raised his hand and said, "Sir, you sound like Genesis."

Parker asked, "What do you mean? Genesis what?"

The reporter answered, "You sound like Genesis in the Bible . . . Let there be light."

Lennox said his friend had never read the Bible but bought one and started to read it. And he couldn't let go of it. It astounded him.

Night after night Parker would read the first chapter of the Bible, Genesis 1. Dr. Lennox said Parker finally contacted him because he knew Lennox was a Christian and would therefore be interested in these things. Parker said, even though he was not religious, he would like to talk with him about science and religion.

The net results? Parker published a book called *The Genesis Enigma: Why the First Book of the Bible Is Scientifically Accurate.*

Parker leads off with a caveat and then continues with this argument:

> "I am not a religious man, and I do not want religion particularly at this time in my life. But what I have discovered is the most remarkable correlation between the order of events as I see them in the history of life and what Genesis says. There's no way the Hebrew writer of Genesis could have known that light was important, that marine life was important."

And then Parker goes through a whole list of points, facts as he knew them to be as a scientist, and then he concludes:

> " . . . the writer of Genesis has it all in the right order. Could this be the evidence of God?"[24]

Lennox says, as brilliant as this book is, it has been rejected by academics primarily because it is so unusual for a scientist who is not a religious man to be so forthright in the correlation of science to the book of Genesis.

So, the origin of life on our planet seems inexplicable for those who live with a godless worldview. The only possible explanation that some try to make is that life has somehow made its way from another planet in another universe. Of course, the question arises: How did life arise on that planet?

The theistic response to the origin of life comes right out of Genesis. In Genesis 1:20-25, God said, "Let the earth sprout vegetation and plants yielding seed." And, then, the Bible says the earth brought forth vegetation. As you keep reading in the first chapter, God did the same with fish in the ocean and birds in the air. He talked about living creatures on Earth, and God spoke and it came into being. He brought into existence something out of nothing.

If there is a God who created the universe, both the heavens and our earth, it seems probable that to bring forth life on this planet would not have been a great challenge for Him.

7.4

Theism's Strongest Argument

When the famous atheist Christopher Hitchens was once asked what was the strongest argument against atheistic belief, he responded:

> "I think every one of us picks the 'fine-tuning' one as the most intriguing...it is not a trivial argument. We (atheists) all say that."[25]

Richard Dawkins, in a conversation with geneticist Dr. Francis Collins, also acknowledged that the fine-tuning of the universe is the most troubling argument that atheists have to deal with.[26]

Dr. Paul Davies, the English physicist, wrote a popular book titled *The Cosmic Blueprint.* Though Davies is considered a religious skeptic, he makes some incredible statements on how the universe is exquisitely fine-tuned and it must be for any conceivable life form to exist. He concludes the book by confessing that the evidence is so overwhelming that there must be someone behind it all, to be able to explain the fine-tuned universe we live in.[27]

Fine-tuning, as it applies to the universe, is the idea that the conditions that allow life to exist in the universe can occur only when certain universal constants lie within a very narrow range of values. If any of several constants were only slightly different, the universe would be unlikely to be conducive to the establishment of life.

All modern scientists agree that the universe seems to be fine-tuned for life. There are so many features in our universe that without which, or if they were slightly different, life could not exist. The universe in which we live gives the appearance of having been designed with incredible precision.

We are told by today's astrophysicists that there were around 122 variables that would need to be lined up with perfect precision in order for our universe to have come into existence. If any of these variables was off by even a million-millionth, matter would not have been able to unite and hold together. There would have been nothing—no stars, no world, no people.[28]

One other major question that skeptics are not able to explain is this: How did the law of physics come into existence? It is one thing to recognize that these 122 variables need to be dialed in with perfect precision, but it's another when you have to explain where these 122 dials came from. They had to exist before the Big Bang itself or else the universe as we know it never would have come into existence.[29]

Stephen Hawking puts the fine-tuning of the universe in these terms:

> "If the overall density of the universe were changed by even 0.0000000000001 percent, no stars or galaxies could be formed. If the rate of expansion one second after the Big Bang had been smaller by even one part in a hundred thousand million million, the universe would have recollapsed before it reached its present size."[30]

This explains why more and more scientists who are atheists are beginning to realize the seriousness of the fine-tuning argument. Astronomer Fred Hoyle was an atheist and a bit of a maverick in the world of science. He was quite shaken when he first examined the evidence of a delicately fine-tuned universe.

He concluded there must be some kind of intelligence behind it all. He uttered these famous words:

> "A common sense interpretation of the facts suggests that a super intellect has monkeyed with physics, as well as with chemistry and biology, and that there are no blind forces worth speaking about in nature."[31]

Even *The Stanford Encyclopedia of Philosophy*, the top secular encyclopedia of philosophy in the world, includes the same claim:

> "The apparent probability of all the necessary conditions sufficient to allow just the formation of planets (let alone life) coming together just by chance is utterly outrageously tiny."[32]

So, if you are a scientist and an atheist, how do you respond to this powerful reality of fine-tuning that no one can dispute?

One way of dealing with it is what Richard Dawkins likes to do and that is to argue that it is only "appearances" of design and purpose. He says that this appearance of design doesn't really exist, because unguided evolution explains it all.

Francis Crick argues along the same lines because he believed people would be misled by the evidence of fine-tuning. So, he issued this warning:

> "Biologists must constantly keep in mind that what they see was not designed, but rather evolved." In other words, he is saying, "Just because it looks like design, don't believe your lying eyes."[33]

However, the evidence is so convincing that Richard Dawkins was asked this in an interview:

> "What do you think is the possibility that intelligent design might turn out to be the answer to some issues in genetics or in evolution?"

And Dawkins responded:

> "Well, it could come about in the following way. It could be that at some earlier time, somewhere in the universe, a civilization evolved...to a very, very high level of technology, and designed a form of life that they seeded onto—perhaps, this planet. Now that is a possibility, and an intriguing possibility. And I suppose it's possible that you might find evidence for that if you look at the details of biochemistry and molecular biology; you might find a signature of some sort of designer."[34]

This seems to be the most popular response to the fine-tuning arguments among skeptics. Stanford University physicist Andrei Linde raises the possibility of our universe being a product of design by some super-technological alien culture. Likewise, astrophysicist John Gribbin says:

> "Serious consideration [should be given to the hypothesis that] our universe is an artificial construct, manufactured deliberately by intelligent beings in another universe."[35]

Dr. Carl Sagan, the renowned astronomer, cosmologist, astrophysicist, and astrobiologist, was also an author and very popular television personality, most famous for his series "Cosmos." He believed that one day extraterrestrials would come to Earth and explain to us the origin of human life. I guess this was more believable to him than a personal God.[36]

I have to be honest that I was shocked when I read these men's explanation for fine-tuning. In one sense, all of these men acknowledge some form of intelligent design from super-intelligent aliens from a far-off universe. However, you have to wonder what type of alien being could fulfill the role of fine-tuner of the universe, and bring the universe into existence.

It seems they do not have a problem believing in some form of intelligent design and designer; they just refuse to believe in God, as the divine intelligent designer.

I sometimes wonder if the problem of the modern skeptic is not that he does not believe in God, but that in his heart of hearts does not want there to be a God. As noted philosopher Thomas Nagel of New York University put it:

> "I want atheism to be true and am made uneasy by the fact that some of the most intelligent and well-informed people I know are religious believers. It isn't just that I don't believe in God and naturally hope there is no God! I don't want there to be a God; I don't want the universe to be like that."[37]

Think about what he said.

> "I want atheism to be true. I don't want there to be a God. I don't want the universe to be like that."

This is a picture of willful blindness, outright unbelief. This is why you have to wonder how much of atheistic belief is in fact a matter of the heart and will, and not of the intellect. I find it interesting what philosopher and scholar Dr. Vince Vitale had to say about those who attribute the possibility of some alien culture for being responsible for the origin of life and the fine-tuning of the universe. He says these types of explanations are cropping up in scholarly literature as an effort to avoid having to admit the existence of God. It is a testimony to the strength of the fine-tuning argument.[38]

7.5

The Mystery of Math

AS I have been performing the research on this book, I have noticed the profound sense of order in our universe as discovered by science. What is so amazing is that the laws of nature have specific mathematical numbers attached to them.

In her wonderful book *Total Truth,* Nancy Pearcey makes this observation:

> "Science offers mathematical formulas to express the cause-and-effect relationships in nature, but that only intensifies the dilemma. For if the universe evolved by blind, material forces acting randomly, why should it fit so neatly into mathematical formulas we invent in our minds? In short, why does math work? In a famous essay titled 'The Unreasonable Effectiveness of Mathematics in the Natural Sciences,' Eugene Wigner says the fact that math works so well in describing the world 'is something bordering on the mysterious.' Indeed, 'there is no rational explanation for it.'

No explanation within scientific materialism, that is. But within the Christian worldview, there is a perfectly rational explanation – namely, that a reasonable God created the world to operate as an orderly progression of events. This was the conviction that inspired the early modern scientists, says math historian Morris

Kline: 'The early mathematicians were sure of the existence of mathematical laws underlying natural phenomena and persisted in the search for them because they were convinced a priori that God had incorporated them in the construction of the universe.'"[39]

When Dr. Francis Collins was a student, he said that Wigner, a Nobel laureate in physics, caught his eye because of the fact that mathematics depicts matter and energy in a very simple and natural way. He then asks:

> "But why should this be? Why should mathematics be so unreasonably effective in describing nature?"[40]

This was such a mystery that the physical world could be described so well mathematically.

It is quite apparent that all of the laws of the universe that have been discovered by science seem to be written in the language of mathematics. It is all so orderly. The world of science finds this to be strange and mysterious.

Physicist Steven Weinberg writes:

> "All my experience as a physicist leads me to believe that there is order in the universe...As we have been going to higher and higher energies and as we have studied structures that are smaller and smaller, we have found that the laws, the physical principles that describe what we learn become simpler and simpler...The rules we have discovered become increasingly coherent and universal...There is a simplicity, a beauty, that we are finding in the rules that govern matter that mirrors something that is built into the logical structure of the universe at a very deep level."[41]

The role of mathematics, which is seamlessly woven into the laws of nature, seems to have been done by deliberate design. It does not seem to be possible that this is a result of blind forces. The popular English physicist Paul Davies, who is a religious agnostic, is deeply impressed by this. He says:

> "It is hard to resist the impression that the present structure of the universe, apparently so sensitive to minor alterations in the numbers, has been rather carefully thought out. The seemingly miraculous concurrence of numerical values that nature has assigned to her fundamental constants must remain the most compelling evidence for an element of cosmic design."[42]

Alexander Tsiaras, an adjunct professor at the Yale Department of Medicine, did a twenty-minute TED Talk presentation with a video on the fetal stages from conception to birth. The video compresses nine months of growth and development into a nine-minute film, and it can be watched on YouTube or on the TED Talk site at the following link:

> https://www.ted.com/talks
> alexander_tsiaras_conception_to_birth_visualized

Tsiaras was very much aware of all the intricacies required to direct this type of project. He says:

> "The complexity of the mathematical models of how these things are done is beyond human comprehension. Even though I am a mathematician, I look at this with marvel: How do these instruction sets not make mistakes as they build what is us? It's a mystery, it's magic, it's divinity."[43]

How is it that the laws of physics and chemistry are articulated in very precise mathematical formulas and equations? Why are nature's laws mathematical? Why is there such mathematical order and not chaos if there is no God? For so many they just throw up their hands and say "It is a mystery."

I, on the other hand, would say that mathematics and the laws of mathematics suggest a divine law giver who arranged the universe to be governed by mathematical laws. As Albert Einstein simply put it: "The mathematical precision of the universe reveals the mathematical mind of God."[44]

In the first century A.D., the apostle Paul wrote in the book of Romans:

> "For since the creation of the world God's invisible qualities—his eternal power and divine nature—have been clearly seen, being understood from what has been made, so that people are without excuse." (Romans 1:20)

More and more people in the world of science are finding Paul's words to be true.

8.

Evolution: A Theory in Crisis

"How do merely physical and mechanical forces—forces without mind, without consciousness—give rise to the world of purposes, thoughts and moral projects? How can a universe of mindless matter produce beings with intrinsic ends [and] self-replication capabilities?"

—ANTONY FLEW

8.1

Darwinian Evolution

THE THEORY of evolution states that the changes in characteristics of a species takes place over many generations and it relies on natural selection to drive the process. Natural selection is the process where an organism is better adapted to its environment and is able to survive and produce more offspring. A phrase often used to describe natural selection is "survival of the fittest." It is the idea that stronger organisms survive, and weaker ones will die out and are eliminated over time. The theory is based on the idea that all species are related and gradually change. The theory of evolution was developed by the English naturalist Charles Darwin and was first put forth in his famous book *On the Origin of Species*, which was first published in 1859.

Not only is the theory of evolution widely believed in the modern world, many presumptuously consider it to be fact and not theory. However, with all the evidence that has been uncovered in the last forty years, many are starting to recognize that the theory of evolution is, in fact, a theory in crisis.

Numerous scholars have come forth and expressed serious doubts about this theory. This included over 700 scientists, all with PhDs, who have signed a declaration of "scientific dissent" from Darwinism evolution. If evolution was a fact, why would there be this type of dissent from so many scientists?[1]

This is why I find it laughable that Richard Dawkins said, "It is absolutely safe to say that if you meet somebody who does not believe in evolution, that person is ignorant, stupid, or insane."

If so much evidence is causing the theory of evolution to be in question, why do so many scientists hold on to it so vigorously?

Nobel laureate Robert Laughlin, who teaches physics at Stanford, had some very profound words on this. He says, "Much of present-day biological knowledge is ideological," and scientists "stop thinking." He goes on to say that Darwinian evolution by natural selection is now functioning more as an anti-theory in an attempt to cover up "embarrassing experimental shortcomings."[2]

The renowned paleontologist Stephen Jay Gould of Harvard was an atheist but clearly rejected Darwin's theory of evolution by natural selection. He says that the ability to prove or disprove the theory is totally inadequate.

This is the problem with evolution. It does not fall into "operational science." There is nothing to be observed, tested, or measured in the laboratory that will validate this theory. The theory of evolution is part of "ongoing science" as we seek to understand the past.

Darwin understood the difficulty in proving the validity of his theory. He recognized that there were so many unanswered questions about evolution, but most significantly he knew that if the emergence of life could not be explained by natural selection, then his entire theory would fall apart. As he himself acknowledged:

> "If it could be demonstrated that any complex organ existed which could not possibly have been formed by numerous, successive, slight modifications, my theory would absolutely break down."[3]

Furthermore, Darwin made it very clear that natural selection's role in the evolution of the species would have to be validated by the fossil record. Darwin understood that if the theory of evolution is indeed true, there must have been a significant number of intermediate links in the fossil record, which would tie all life forms together.

However, with great humility and integrity, Darwin ultimately had to acknowledge that there was no great fossil evidence that had yet been found during his lifetime. He believed, however, that future fossil discoveries would vindicate his theory. And a new branch of science, the forensic science of paleontology, developed the tools and the methods to study the fossil record as it was discovered and developed.

Before we consider the fossil record, I think it is important to know that when the term evolution is used, we need to recognize that there are two types of evolution.

First, there's microevolution—changes that take place within a species that has been observed to be true, as seen, for example, in dogs or cats. And second is macroevolution. This theory claims that all living creatures have a common ancestor and that natural selection brought forth the development of every one of the countless organisms we see in the modern world, all from a single life form.

This is important because it explains how Darwin came up with his theory. He spent five years on the Galapagos Islands, where he carefully studied the beaks of finches. He watched the beaks of certain species of finches grow wider while others got longer. This occurred in response to varying available food. Darwin concluded he was observing natural selection at work, as these changes in beak sizes helped the finches survive. However, he was watching microevolution at work within a species, which happens quite often. Biologists have now been observing these finches for 150 years. There have been no dramatic changes in them at all other than beak size, which vary around a certain mean.[4]

8.2

The Fossil Record

DARWIN CAME up with the term "intermediate linkage," which he believed would have to be found throughout the fossil record if the theory of evolution was to be validated. For instance, there would have to be intermediate forms between apes and early man. If you put apes (or, more particularly, according to current theory, chimpanzees) on one side of the room and human beings (Homo sapiens) on the other, then, between these two, there should be a direct intermediate linkage to an intermediate species, our remote ancestor. As children, we generally label this linkage a "caveman," but in the science of anthropology we speak of pre-humans with such names as Neanderthal or Australopithecus, early primate species continually evolving, in stepped gradations, leading to Cro-Magnon man, the first early human.

But why are there no surviving prehistoric ancestors? We have apes and we have humans, but there are no living intermediate linkages alive today. And this same absence of intermediate linkages goes for other species, too. Where are they? Supposedly, having died out, they must be somewhere in the fossil record?

The truth is that human scientists have been searching for our prehistoric ancestors in the fossil record since the mid-1800s. The reasonable question to ask is: How are they doing?

Well, apparently, not that well.

Lee Strobel, whom I mention earlier, was drawn to atheism because of what he was taught in biology class in high school. He went on a two-year investigation for the truth of life and, during his search, remained a believer in Darwinian theory. However, as he progressed, he became deeply troubled by the lack of fossil evidence for the intermediate links between the varied species.

Here are some examples of the types of observations he encountered. This first one is from a college textbook titled, *General Paleontology.*

> "One of the most surprising negative results of paleontological research in the last century is that such transitional forms seem to be inordinately scarce. In Darwin's time this could perhaps be ascribed to the incompleteness of the paleontological record and to the lack of knowledge. But with the enormous number of fossil species, which have been discovered since then, other causes must be found for the almost complete absence of transitional forms."[5]

David Raup, a highly regarded paleontologist at the University of Chicago and the curator of the Field Museum of Natural History in Chicago, said:

> "We are now about 150 years after Darwin, and the knowledge of the fossil record has been greatly expanded. We now have a quarter of a million fossil species, but the situation hasn't changed much. We have even fewer examples of evolutionary transition than we had in Darwin's time."[6]

T.S. Kemp, an Oxford zoologist, writes:

> "Paleontology, certainly as much as any other branch of biology, and perhaps more than most, is prone to speculation. This consists of ideas that cannot be falsified, because suit-

> able methods for testing them are simply not available."[7]

And probably the most influential evolutionary biologist of the twentieth century, the late Stephen Jay Gould of Harvard, says this:

> " . . . the extreme rarity of transitional forms in the fossil record persists as the trade secret of paleontology. The evolutionary trees that adorn our textbooks have data only at the tips and nodes of their branches. The rest is inference, however reasonable, not the evidence of fossils...Darwin's argument that the geological record is extremely imperfect, still persists as the favored escape of most paleontologists from the embarrassment of a record that seems to show so little evidence of evolution."[8]

The late David B. Kitts, School of Geology and Geophysics, Department of the History of Science, University of Oklahoma, offered the following cautionary advice:

> "Despite the bright promise that paleontology provides a means of "seeing" evolution, it has presented some nasty difficulties for evolutionists, the most notorious of which is the presence of "gaps" in the fossil record. Evolution requires intermediate forms between species, and paleontology does not provide them."[9]

The late Dr. Colin Patterson, former Senior Paleontologist at the British Museum of Natural History, stated:

> "I will lay it on the line—there is not one such fossil for which one could make a watertight argument."[10]

Dr. David Pilbeam is a distinguished paleontologist and is Professor of Anthropology at Harvard. He admits:

> "Perhaps generations of students of human evolution, including myself, have been flailing about in the dark." He goes on to say, "There is no clear-cut and inexorable pathway from ape to man."[11]

Dr. D.V. Ager was a paleontologist and president of the British Geological Association. He said:

> "It must be significant that nearly all the evolutionary stories I learned as a student have now been debunked."[12]

Most significantly, the late aerospace engineer Luther D. Sutherland, in his book *Darwin's Enigma: Fossils and Other Problems,* describes interviews that he conducted with five of the leading paleontologists in the world, all who worked at prestigious natural history museums. Each of these museums had extensive fossil collections. According to Sutherland:

> "None of the five museum officials could offer a single example of a transitional series of fossilized organisms that would document the transformation of one basically different type to another."[13]

Niles Eldredge is a very highly regarded biologist and paleontologist and, for many years, has been on the staff of the American Museum of Natural History in New York. He said something quite remarkable about natural selection and the theory of gradual adaptive change:

> "We paleontologists have said that the history of life supports…[the story of adaptive change]...all the while knowing that it does not."[14]

Eldredge and his good friend Dr. Stephen Gould are considered two of the most prominent paleontologists ever to live. Paleontology, if you will remember, is the study of fossils and the fossil record. From their work, they realized that Darwinian evolution of slow change was in trouble. Yet they recognized that Darwinism was the "official" position that Western evolutionists clung to. The two of them, however, abandoned this "official" position because there was no evidence to support it in the fossil record.[15]

Therefore Gould, Eldredge, and a host of other scientists have renounced Darwinism for a new theory of evolution called "punctuated equilibrium," which holds that evolutionary transitions occur rapidly and not slowly as Darwin insisted. And Gould says this is why modern humans have such little chance of finding our ancestor primates in the fossil record. These transitions take place because of catastrophes in nature—volcanoes, asteroids, droughts, floods—and they happen so quickly relative to a geologic span of time.

I am finding that so many people who believe in evolution have no idea the fossil record is almost void of any transitional forms that Darwin insisted must be found to validate his theory.

As you can see, there are many holes in evolutionary theory, particularly in the fossil record. Darwin was quite clear when he admitted this hole in the fossil record is "the most obvious and gravest objection which can be argued against my theory."

Darwin would be the first to admit that if the fossil record could not validate natural selection, then the theory of evolution would collapse. Nevertheless, people cling to this theory, primarily, I believe, because it is the foundation of their atheistic worldview.

8.3
What About Cavemen?

I REMEMBER seeing as a kid—and you probably have seen this, too—an illustration in the *World Book* Encyclopedia. On the far left was an ape-like creature, and, next to this creature, moving to the right, you would see a succession of other ape-looking creatures along a timeline. Finally, at the end of the timeline, you would see a human being.

This means of illustrating evolution was an innovation of the American Museum of Natural History. And the second prehistoric man in line, after the ape, is who they call Java Man. You may have heard of Java Man because he was the first human fossil discovered in 1891 by Dutch scientist Eugene Dubois. It was a huge discovery at the time, as many believed this was the missing link between apes and humans.

It was many years later, though, that the true story was discovered. Java Man merely consists of nothing more than a skullcap, a single femur, or thigh bone, and three teeth…and a great imagination on the part of Dubois. This is what Lee Strobel has to say about Dubois' supposed discovery.

> "As a youngster beginning to form my opinions about human evolution, I wasn't aware of what I have more recently discovered that Dubois' shoddy excavation would have disqualified the fossil from consideration by today's standards.

> Or that the femur bone didn't really belong with the skullcap. Or that the skullcap, according to prominent Cambridge University anatomist Sir Arthur Keith, was distinctly human and reflected a brain capacity well within the range of humans living today. Or, that a 342-page scientific report from a fact-finding expedition of nineteen evolutionists demolished Dubois' claims and concluded that Java Man played no part in human evolution. In short, Java Man was not an ape-man as I'd been led to believe, but he was a true member of the human family."[16]

He says this was a fact apparently lost on *Time* magazine, which, as recently as 1994, treated Java Man as a legitimate evolutionary ancestor.

And then there appears to be credible evidence of a striking, almost unbelievable level of fraud (or, as seen in the best light, incompetence) in the creation of the actual number and identification of the fossils themselves.

Investigative science journalists need to focus on how representative the fossil record is in terms of numbers of complete sets of life forms, the actual count of bones and complete skeletons. How many full, complete human skeletons do we have? And how complete and accurate is the science when reconstructing various life forms simply from a few bones?

Most of us are not aware that anthropologists might find a jawbone or a skull or some teeth, and then will reconstruct a skeleton of what they think it would look like. They rarely disclose the fact that their conclusion, which is usually presented via the media in the form of an artist's rendering, has been based solely, for example, on one small part of a skull and one femur and a few digits from the left hand. (This is like having a police sketch of a criminal on the loose . . . except in these cases we have actual eyewitnesses; or like a rendering of a murder victim from just one or two bone fragments...except in these cases the renderings are consistently problematic, questionable, and seldom lead to an actual identification.)

In 1985, Richard Leakey, the famous paleontologist, was a guest on "The Dick Cavett Show." Leakey had with him some impressive-looking human fossils. As they were talking about the fossils, Cavett continues to press Leakey gently about how many of the bones were actually found in the ground.

Well, Leakey finally admitted, actually just a small piece of bone was found and then he and his team of experts reconstructed the rest with plaster. Cavett was dumbfounded.

Naturally, whenever you read about these great fossil finds, you assume it's this well-preserved ancient human skeleton. British paleontologist Henry Gee, who's the senior science writer for the prestigious *Nature* magazine, said this:

> "The intervals of time that separate fossils are so huge that we cannot say anything definite about their possible connection through ancestry and descent."

Gee called each fossil an isolated point with no knowledgeable connection to any other given fossil, and they all float around in an overwhelming sea of gaps. In fact, he said:

> "All the fossil evidence for human evolution between ten and five million years ago, several thousand generations of living creatures, can be fitted into a small box."[17]

There are many more stories like this that took place in the twentieth century and were highly celebrated in the news and among paleontologists that, in the end, proved to be fraudulent.

- In 1922, a single tooth unearthed in Nebraska was enthusiastically claimed to be from an early type of Pithecanthrope (ape-like man) who lived between 1.7 and 5.5 million years ago. *The Illustrated London News* published a double-page feature trumpeting Nebraska Man as a vital link in the 'monkey to man' chain, but six years later it was discovered that the tooth had come from a peccary, a pig-like wild animal. The Nebraska Man claim now shares the peccary's state of extinction, but together they are a good illustration of the comment made by Professor Bolton Davidheiser of Johns Hopkins University: 'The non-scientific public has great faith in what a paleontologist can do with a single bone.'[18]

- In 1959, the well-known paleontologist Louis Leakey and his wife, Mary, exhumed an interesting skull in East Africa. Dubbed 'Nutcracker Man' because of its huge jaw, it was first dated at 1.75 million years, making it by far the oldest hominid fossil ever found, but this claim was torpedoed when further bones found lower down were dated at only just over 10,000 years. Leakey eventually withdrew his extravagant claim and conceded that his find was one of many Australopithecus africanus, now believed to be extinct African apes.

- In 1974 the American anthropologist Donald Johanson found a tiny skeleton east of the Great Rift Valley, Ethiopia. Nicknamed 'Lucy,' it was dated at three million years and became a sensation when announced at the Nobel Symposium on Early Man in 1978. Lucy was hailed as the first ape to walk upright and an undoubted link between apes and humans, but in a question-and-answer session at the University of Missouri in 1996, Johanson admitted that the knee joint cited as proof that Lucy walked upright had been found more than two miles away and 200 feet lower in the strata! Richard Leakey, Director of Kenya's National Museum, decided that 'the evidence for the alleged transformation from ape to man is extremely unconvincing,' and that 'it is overwhelmingly likely that Lucy was no more than a variety of pygmy chimpanzee.' Johanson eventually withdrew his original claim and concluded that Lucy was not related to humans at all.[19]

The Wall Street Journal in October 2011 ran a book review titled "Bones That Tell a Tale," presenting some compelling information from *The Fossil Chronicles,* a book by Dean Falk. The reviewer, Brian Switek, suggests that seldom has the discovery of an ancient human fossil ever been announced without stirring immediate controversy. He says for more than 150 years, revelations of a new species of our prehistoric kin have sent scientists into a tizzy about the meaning of the news. In his book review, Switek informs us that only a short while before his review ran in *The Wall Street Journal,* another source, *Science Magazine,* has announced the existence of two million-year-old "human-like" fossils found in a South African cave, yet no one has yet to agree on how this "ancestor" of ours actually relates to us. And the article goes on to say that every time there's a new fossil discovery, there seems always to be a huge dispute over what it actually represents. The principal reason? The fossil find doesn't add up, consisting of maybe a little bone, a jaw, maybe a skull . . . and that's about it.[20]

It seems as if paleontologists all over the world are desperately trying to find an ancient human fossil that will prove to be the intermediate linkage between apes and man. However, after 150 years of searching for this missing link, no one wants to admit that maybe it doesn't exist.

8.4

The Mystery of the Human Eye

William Paley was an English philosopher who lived in the late 1700s and died in 1805. He believed that God was a master craftsman, similar to a person who assembles a watch or a telescope. To help people understand this, he presented to his friends the similarities of the human eye with a high-powered telescope. This is what he determined:

- The eye was made for vision; the telescope was made for assisting it.
- Each uses a sophisticated lens to achieve its function and purpose.
- Both reflect and manipulate light.
- Both are able to bring an object into proper focus. The muscles surrounding the soft lens of the eye move to bring objects into focus, while a telescope uses dials to move the lens.

With this in mind, he asked his friends if it would be reasonable to believe that the telescope was created by a craftsman while the eye was not. Should they not both be considered products of design?[21]

I mention Paley's illustration because natural selection has a difficult time accounting for the human eye. Darwin clearly recognized that understanding how the eye was formed posed a problem to his theory, as he wrote bluntly in a letter:

> "The eye to this day gives me a cold shudder."[22]

The complexity of the eye causes problems for evolutionary theory because a biological system like the eye had to develop over millions of years, and would have never worked until fully developed.

Darwin clearly saw this as a real problem.

The August 15, 2005, cover story of *Time* magazine was "Evolution Wars." It was a fairly lengthy article on the theory of evolution versus the theory of intelligent design. It addressed this thorny issue of the human eye. It would be very difficult for the eye to be the product of accidental mutations. As Michael Behe, an American biochemist, asks, "How could a process of gradual improvements produce a complex organ that needs all its parts—pinhole, lens, light-sensitive surface—in order to work?" Behe says the eye closely resembles a camera, which is clearly a product that someone has designed.[23]

The tiny retina of the eye has 130 million receptor cells, 124 million of which are rod shaped and enable us to differentiate between light and darkness. Six million of these receptor cells are cone shaped and can identify up to eight million variations of color. Could this really occur by a random, purposeless process?

Author John Blanchard makes a significant point:

> "A partial eye is useless. Five percent of an eye would not give five percent vision—it would give none. What is more, even if all the physical components of an eye were in place, they would achieve nothing unless they were precisely 'wired' to an amazing complex of nerve cells in the brain. Small wonder that someone has suggested, 'Examination of the eye is a cure for atheism.'"[24]

Dr. Ming Wang is a world-renowned eye surgeon who earned

his MD from Harvard and his PhD in laser physics from MIT. He is one of the few LASIK surgeons in the world who holds a doctorate in laser physics. He has performed over fifty-five thousand cataract and LASIK procedures, including more than four thousand on fellow doctors.

Wang grew up in China and moved to the United States in 1982. In his years at Harvard and MIT he was an atheist. However, over time as he considered the human brain and how it was assembled, he began to question his atheistic belief. He says:

> "As a medical doctor and a scientist, I can firmly attest to the fact that it is impossible for natural selection to form the intricacies of the eye."[25]

Over time, he became a Christian because he could not find in science answers to those questions in life that he had been searching for. He said:

> "The more I learned about science, the more—not less—evidence that I saw of God's creation and design. For example, as I was becoming an ophthalmologist and learning about the inner workings of the eye, the amazing and logical arrangement of photoreceptors, ganglion cells, and neurons, I realized that there is absolutely no way that an intricate structure such as the human eye could ever evolve from a random compilation of cells. The very complexity of a human eye is, in fact, the most powerful evidence of the existence of God."[26]

This is a very powerful argument particularly since Darwin himself saw that the complexity of the eye had the potential to completely undermine his theory.

8.5

Simple Mathematics

BACK IN 2013, I wrote a book titled *Reliable Truth: The Validity of the Bible in an Age of Skepticism.* In an effort to get my hands around this whole issue of man's first appearance in the world and what science can teach us about human life, I undertook a study on the history of the population of the world. After my initial survey of the resources available to me, I turned to the Population Reference Bureau. They work in conjunction with the United Nations and have produced a chart that purports to be an estimated history of the human population.

In 2009, there were 6.7 billion people on Earth. In 1974, there were 4 billion. In 1927, there were 2 billion, and in 1804, 1 billion. As we get down to around 1500, the report indicates that they cannot tell us much more—as this is just an estimate, it states that there were approximately 500 million people alive in the year 1500.

YEAR	POPULATION
1500	500,000,000
1804	1,000,000,000
1927	2,000,000,000
1974	4,000,000,000
2009	6,700,000,000

You can see this doubling taking place. The concept of "doubling time" is the period of time required for a quantity to double in size or value. It can be used for such things as bacterial growth and population studies, compound interest and tumors. So, I decided to extrapolate backwards down the timeline. According to my estimate, it takes roughly twenty-eight doubling generations, as you go back in time, until you would eventually end up with just two people. That's it.

So, the question is: Who were these two people?

The first option is that the first two people were created by God. Genesis 1:27 says, "God created man in His own image."

You also see God's ability to create through the life of Jesus. For example, Christ transforms water into wine at a wedding celebration. He takes a couple of fish and loaves of bread and created enough food to feed more than five thousand people. And then He approaches a man, Lazarus, who had been dead for four days, his corpse decaying, and He breathes life into him saying, "Come forth!" out of the grave.

So the first option to consider is the biblical message that God created the first man, Adam, and the first woman, Eve.

Of course, the second option is that two pre-human primates, male and female, evolved over millions of years and became the "Cro-Magnons," the first *Homo sapiens.*

Those are the two options.

While I was researching this information, there was this caveat attached to the Population Bureau's study suggesting that the set of specific characteristics that define a human is "a matter of definition." It is open to debate over which members of early Homo sapiens should be considered human. Even if the scientific community reached wide consensus regarding which characteristics distinguished human beings, it merely would be to pinpoint the time of their first appearance as the fossil record is simply too sparse. This, of course, is no surprise.

Which raises, I think, the necessary question: When did the first Cro-Magnon man and woman go from being animals to being two self-aware human beings? When did they become designed in the image of God? When did they go from being animals to human beings that have souls? And, more importantly, when did they develop consciousness, an awareness of their self, and their individuality?

Over the years, I have always believed God initiated creation, but I have been ambivalent about the Adam and Eve story. I always wondered if it was not some type of allegory.

However, over time, by faith, I have concluded that God supernaturally created Adam and Eve. I think it is very believable if God exists. It is also much more believable than the evolution account, particularly when you see there is no fossil record to support it. Finally, Adam is mentioned nine times in the New Testament.

However, there are a great number of men and women (such as scientist Francis Collins) who believe that God created everything in the beginning and life has evolved into what we see in the world today. It's called theistic evolution, with God's presence invested in each new life, in every generation from the beginning of time. I don't believe this is the means God has chosen, but some Christians do. What we can all agree on, however, is that we exist and God stands behind our existence, and as human beings, we reflect His glory.

Several times in my research, I encountered a scientist named James Tour. He's a professor in the department of chemistry at the Center for Nanoscale Science and Technology at Rice University. He has a doctorate in organic chemistry from Purdue, and he has done post-doctoral work at Stanford and the University of Wisconsin. Tour is on the cutting edge of research in the molecular world and has written more than 140 technical research articles and holds seventeen U.S. patents. He says this:

> "I build molecules for a living...I can't begin to tell you how difficult that job is."

In a speech several years ago, he described something he realized as he probed deeper and deeper into the awe-inspiring wonders at the molecular level.

> "I stand in awe of God because of what He has done through His creation...Only a rookie who knows nothing about science would say science takes away from faith. If you really study science, it will bring you closer to God."[27]

Wherever we reach, from the smallest particle to the largest galaxy, from the alpha to the omega, in the room where we are reading these very words to the great natural world outside, we will find, if we seek, the fingerprints of an intelligent designer. Generations of brilliant men and women from the dawn of time have been led on this quest by the intimations of God in the details. The deep mysteries of life, of emotions, of love and death—all, perhaps, can be studied and broken down into smaller and smaller components by the scientific method, but in the process, the inklings of a creative force should always surprise us with awe and wonder.

8.6

A Scientist Changes His Mind

IT SEEMS that more and more people whose lives are steeped in the sciences are discovering that Darwinian evolution is not consistent with their own research. This is what Dr. Michael Egnor encountered in his research as a pediatric neurosurgeon.

He had developed an atheistic worldview after years of rigorous scientific training. What is so fascinating is how it was actually through science that he discovered how mistaken he had been. He says, "I was raised as an agnostic and grew up pretty much as a scientific materialist." In his mind, Christianity was nothing more than fictional stories that taught moral lessons.

He felt very strongly about his worldview because, in his mind, science had decisively disproved the existence of God. He said,

> "As a science major in college, I was steeped in Darwinian evolution, which seemed to demonstrate that life could be explained perfectly well by material mechanisms alone. There was no reason to invoke God."

In his mind, Darwin's theory seemed to have discredited the argument for intelligent design.

Dr. Egnor also studied Freud, who convinced him that God is nothing more than "wish fulfillment," the desperate search for a father figure. He said, "Every time I ever considered Christianity, I was stopped cold by the thought it would mean abandoning scientific integrity."

Over time, Egnor was wildly successful, rising to the top of his field. He was appointed professor and vice president of neurosurgery at State University of New York, Stony Brook. *New York Magazine* named him one of New York's best doctors in 2005. He developed a theory of blood flow to the brain. It was through his research that his perspective began to change. He was surprised to find that the cranial system, which he was studying, was like a delicately and ingeniously designed gadget. There is a filter that protects the delicate capillaries from the powerful force of the heartbeat. He said:

> "It is a finely tuned mechanism analogous to vibration dampers widely used in engineering. In fact, most of what I needed to know was not in biology textbooks but in engineering textbooks."

Of course, engineering is all about design.

It began to dawn on Egnor that virtually all of his biological research operates on the presumption of design. Biologists, for instance, have a procedure called "reverse engineering." It is as if you are working (backwards) to reproduce the engineer's thought process. However, in biology, there is no engineer; there is no designer. Biology teaches that nature is the product of the random and mindless process of natural selection.

In Egnor's work as a medical researcher, he continued to run into the same problem. His research contradicted his belief in Darwinian evolution. He said:

> "I was surprised at how little the Darwinian paradigm contributed to my work. By contrast, the design paradigm aligned nicely with the most important aspects of my research."

He recognized that he had come to a point where a decision

needed to be made. What does one do when his theory is contradicted by the facts? As a man of integrity, he followed the truth. He concluded that the reason living things appeared and function as if they were designed is because they were designed. He said:

> "I came to see that Darwinism is a philosophical bias more than a coherent science. Darwinian processes may explain some patterns and changes in gene frequency in populations, but the evidence does not even remotely support the claim that chance and necessity fully account for the appearance of complex design in living things."[28]

Egnor abandoned his belief in Darwinian evolution because he respected the evidence he had encountered, and consequently, he made the decision to become a Christian. In the process, he discovered immediately a new sense of unity and wholeness. He had found a new worldview that was in harmony with his research, and with the real world in which he lives.

8.7

Stubborn Resistance in Evolutionary Theory

ONE OF the most baffling observations I have made in researching the theory of evolution is how so many scientists tenaciously hold on to this theory in the face of so much evidence that undermines it. You would think they might consider Gould's theory of punctuated equilibrium. Clearly, some are turning to the possibility of a multi-universe where life and the first human beings were placed here by alien beings.

Dr. Richard Lewontin is an evolutionary biologist, a mathematician, and a geneticist who is now retired but taught for many years at Harvard. Though an atheist, he made some fascinating remarks in *The New York Review of Books.* These words have been quoted in many of the research books I've read (emphasis mine):

> "Our willingness to accept scientific claims that are against common sense is the key to an understanding of the real struggle between science and the supernatural. We take the side of science in spite of the patent absurdity of some of its constructs, in spite of its failure to fulfill many of its extravagant promises of health and life, in spite of the tolerance of the scientific community for unsubstantiated just-so stories, because *we have a prior commitment to materialism.* It is not that the methods and institutions of science somehow compel us

> to accept a material explanation of the phenomenal world but, on the contrary, that *we are forced by our* a priori *adherence to material causes* to create an apparatus of investigation and a set of concepts that produce material explanations, no matter how counterintuitive, no matter how mystifying to the uninitiated. Moreover, that materialism is absolute for *we cannot allow a divine foot in the door.*"[29]

Think about what he has said. It is an incredible admission that Darwinists have accepted certain scientific claims that go against common sense. He acknowledges that scientists take the side of science even though some of its theories and constructs are absurd. They accept so many unsubstantiated stories because of their commitment to atheistic materialism. Most significantly he makes it clear "we cannot allow a divine foot in the door."

But what if there is a divine intelligence that brought all of this into existence? Are you going to refuse to accept the truthfulness of it because you are committed to atheism though you know it to be false? This is a picture of willful blindness being taken to an extreme.

This helps us better understand why so many Darwinian scientists cling to this entrenched dogma that is jealously guarded and immune to all criticism. You have to ask yourself, "Where is the intellectual integrity?" If God exists, are you saying we cannot let Him in the door?

Dr. David Berlinski, a mathematician with his PhD from Princeton, also an agnostic, believes strongly that scientific atheism offers an incoherent understanding of the universe and how we arrived here on Earth. He has written some scorching words that expose the real motivation behind scientists' attempt to avoid the theistic implications on the beginning of the universe. He states emphatically that physicists seek to avoid believing in a theistic beginning because it is emotionally unacceptable. For this reason they have made every effort to find an alternative. He then sarcastically asks, if you thought scientists were completely committed to pursuing the truth, "Well, you were wrong."[30]

If you will recall, Richard Dawkins is probably the boldest and most outspoken defender of Darwinism in the world. If you remember, he said if you did not believe in evolution, you are either ignorant, stupid, or insane. He, however, on another occasion acknowledged this:

> "Even if there were no actual evidence in favor of Darwinian theory…we should still be justified in preferring it over all rival theories."[31]

Are you kidding me? You would even be willing to believe it without any evidence whatsoever? It seems this is what actually has happened.

Even though Dawkins has been known to promote evolution strongly as a fact, he seems to backtrack when he tries to explain the fine-tuning of the universe. He admits that life on our planet may have come from an alien universe.

Dr. Rodney Stark has an interesting observation of all of this. Stark is an American sociologist and a long-time professor of sociology and comparative religion. Stark makes it clear he is neither an evolutionist nor a proponent of intelligent design. He regards himself as a scholar who pursues historical evidence. He did an in-depth study on the conflict between evolution and intelligent design. The study was published by Princeton Press, and Stark concludes that this is not a clash where scientists have had to fend off the attack of religious fanatics. He says from the very start:

> "It has primarily been an attack on religion by militant atheists who wrap themselves in the mantle of science in an effort to refute all religious claims concerning a Creator—an effort that has also often attempted to suppress all scientific criticism of Darwin's work."[32]

Stark also points out that the research is clear that Darwin was aware of the deficiencies in his own theory. Darwin recognized that he could never establish that natural selection took place in all the various species. So many of his breeding experiments fell short. He was the first to recognize that gradual change in nature was essential to his theory, yet there was no evidence for it. This is when he acknowledged that in order to prove his theory to be true, the proof would be in the fossil record. However, the evidence in the fossil record is still missing.

Stark concludes, after examining all of the Darwinist arguments, the "Darwinian theory does rest on truly miraculous assumptions."[33]

There is a good reason so many cling to this theory: Clearly it is the foundation of their atheistic worldview. Richard Dawkins admitted this when he said that Darwin "made it possible to be an intellectually fulfilled atheist." He is acknowledging that atheism has no intellectual credibility apart from evolution. They are faced with the fact that the universe has a beginning and therefore a cause, they have no explanation whatsoever how life originated on this planet, and the collapse of Darwinian evolution would be their demise. It is no wonder they have such fanatical fervor for this theory that clearly is in crisis.

9.

The Existence of God

"My faith is not built on arguments of logic and reason; it is built on revelation."

FYODOR DOSTOYEVSKY

9.1

Does God Have a Name?

IF THE evidence points to the existence of a transcendent infinite spiritual force in the universe, this force will remain unknown to us unless it appears and reveals its identity. The human search for God will always be an effort in futility, unless God chooses to reveal Himself in a convincing manner.

As we survey the host of world religions, I am convinced there is only one place to start and that is with the historical figure Jesus Christ.

Jesus is the only credible figure in history who made the claim to be God. In his book *The Everlasting Man,* G.K. Chesterton pointed out that no great moral teacher ever claimed to be God—not Mohammed, not Micah, not Malachi, or Confucius or Plato or Moses or Buddha:

> "Not one of them ever made that claim…and the greater the man is, the less likely he is to make the very greatest claim."[1]

C.S. Lewis made this insightful observation:

> "If you had gone to Buddha and asked him, 'Are you the son of Brahman?' he would have said, 'My son, you are still in the vale of illusion.' If you had gone to Socrates and asked, 'Are you Zeus?' he would have laughed at you. If you had

> gone to Mohammed and asked, 'Are you Allah?' he would first have rent his clothes and then cut your head off...The idea of a great moral teacher saying what Christ said is out of the question."[2]

For many years, the brilliant British scholar Malcolm Muggeridge was an outspoken atheist. One of the reasons he eventually changed his mind was because of the man Jesus. He said that plenty of great teachers, mystics, martyrs, and saints have made their appearance at different times in the world, having lived lives and spoken words full of grace and truth for which we have reason to be grateful. Nevertheless, Muggeridge continues, man needs God's special revelation on which he can build a religious belief and from which he can find wisdom and understanding. Muggeridge goes on to say that the only solution is for God to become man, which He did through the Incarnation in the person of Jesus Christ. God thereby:

> "set a window in the dark dungeons of our soul," that He might "let in a light which would provide a view, and offer a way to be released from the misery of our self-centeredness and pride." In Jesus, "eternity steps into time, and time loses itself in eternity."[3]

So, Jesus must be the place to start in a search for God, because of His incredible claim to be God. It seems only logical to seek to determine if His claims were true. The essays in this final section will provide the compelling evidence that Jesus is Who He claims to be.

However, I need to mention a second reason that Jesus and Christianity is where a person should start in his search for spiritual truth. Christianity is the only falsifiable religion in the world. The reason I say this is because Christianity depends on certain historical facts to be true. (This, of course, would include Christ's Resurrection.) Prove they never happened and Christianity is fraudulent.

Probably one of the most respected books on man's diverse spiritual longings is *The World's Religions* by Huston Smith. Written in 1958, it is still used regularly in many college curriculums. Commentator Bill Moyers suggests it is one of the best books on comparative religion because of its objectivity and its sensitivity to all religious beliefs and practices. Smith, who was very well educated, didn't have any particular religious leaning. He was unbiased. And in the book, in the section on Christianity, he begins with these words:

> "Christianity is basically a historical religion. That is to say, it is founded not on abstract principles but in concrete events, actual historical happenings."[4]

Out of all the religions that Smith covers, he doesn't say this about any of the other world religions. The Bible, he suggests, unlike most of the world's great religious literature and traditions, is not centered on a series of moral, spiritual, and liturgical teachings but rather on what God did in history and what He revealed in history.

The historical record does not seem to be of as much importance in other world religions. For instance, a number of years ago, theologian Paul Tillich hosted a conference in Asia with various Buddhist thinkers. During the conference he asked a simple question: What if by some fluke Siddhārtha Gautama, the Buddha, had never lived and turned out to be some sort of fabrication? What would be the implications for Buddhism? The scholars all agreed that if Buddha had not existed, it would not matter. The reason, they concluded, is because Buddhism should be judged as an abstract philosophy, a system for living. They said it did not matter where the teaching originated.[5]

Christianity, on the other hand, requires an origination, a set of hard facts on which to stand. To make the point more explicitly, Peter Moore, the founder of Trinity School for Ministry, emphasizes that Christianity is the only world religion to make spiritual truth depend on historical events. And English historian and author Paul Johnson bolsters this truth by stating the following:

> "Christianity is essentially a historical religion. It bases its claims on the historical facts it asserts. If these are demolished it is nothing."[6]

Therefore, Christians clearly believe that as wonderful as Jesus's life and teachings were, they are meaningless if they are not historically true.

One of my favorite stories is of a man who believed he could debunk the Christian story by diligent study of the historical and archeological record.

Sir William Mitchell Ramsay is considered to be one of the greatest archeologists in history. He performed most of his work across Asia Minor and the Middle East. An Englishman, he was raised an atheist, the son of atheists of great wealth. Receiving his doctorate in archeology from Oxford, he committed his entire life to archeology and set out for the Holy Land with the intention of undermining the validity of the Bible. His hope was completely to discredit the book of Acts. He was confident he could do so because there was simply so much historical information he believed he could draw upon.

> "I began with a mind unfavorable to it [Acts] . . . It did not lie then in my line of life to investigate the subject matter minutely; but more recently I found myself often brought into contact with the book of Acts as an authority for the topography, antiquities, and society of Asia Minor."

Over time, Ramsay was forced to reverse completely his beliefs as a result of the overwhelming evidence uncovered in his research. After thirty years of vigorous and comprehensive study and analysis, this is what he had to say about Luke's ability as a historian:

> "Luke is a historian of the first rank; not merely are his statements as facts trustworthy . . . this author should be placed along with the greatest of historians . . . Luke's history is unsurpassed in respect to its trustworthiness."[7]

These are strong words and are of vital importance. Remember the foundational principle we started with at the beginning of this chapter? Christianity is the only world religion where spiritual truth depends on the veracity of clearly defined and discoverable historical events.

Eventually, after uncovering many hundreds of artifacts confirming the historicity of the New Testament record, Ramsay would shock the archaeological community when he revealed to the world that he had become a Christian.[8]

9.2

Jesus: A Historical Figure?

AS HARD as this might be to believe, there are some people convinced that Jesus was not a man of history but some type of mythical figure. They claim the Resurrection story was based on ancient myths of religious figures who rose from the dead. These mythological stories were written many years before the Christian myth was written. However, there are no credible historical scholars who make this claim.

In the wonderful book *The Story of Reality*, Greg Koukl confronts this issue head on. He has read extensively from the trained historians who have gone back to the earliest records of these ancient accounts. Here is what those historians have discovered.

- A close look at the primary sources shows two things that are startling given the popularity of this view. First, the myths that actually *pre-date* Jesus' time bear virtually no resemblance to the particular details of Jesus' life. A host of alleged similarities turn out to be nonexistent. Whatever parallels remain are usually far too general to be significant.

- According to historian Tryggve Mettinger, the scholar who has done the most recent exhaustive study of this question, there simply is *"no prima facie"* evidence that the death and Resurrection of Jesus is a mythological construct, drawing on the myths and rites of the dying and rising gods of the surrounding world.

- Second, mythical accounts of the mystery-religion gods that actually do bear some resemblance to Jesus' life unfortunately (for the theory) show up *after* his time. This fact creates a problem for the recycled redeemer view since it looks very much like those stories were copied from the Gospels, not the other way around. Clearly, the child cannot come before the parent. The "recycled" version must appear in the historical record *after* the one it allegedly came from, not *before it*.[9]

It is also important to recognize the number of ancient historians, who lived during the time of Christ, and wrote of Him.

Historian Gary Habermas details a total of thirty-nine ancient sources documenting the life of Christ. Some of these were Christian historians, but many of them were not. To put this into perspective, there are only nine ancient sources that mention Tiberius Caesar. Only nine. Here we find an emperor of Rome who ruled for twenty-two years, yet there are only nine ancient sources that mention him while there are thirty-nine sources that speak of Jesus. Of these thirty-nine, several mention Jesus in just a paragraph or two while others write of him extensively.[10]

These include Cornelius Tacitus, considered the greatest historian of the Roman Empire who was born in 57 A.D., and Justin Martyr, who lived from 65 A.D. to 110 A.D. and wrote extensively of Jesus. Then you have Flavius Josephus, touted as the greatest Jewish historian of antiquity and who wrote about the life of Christ. He was born in 37 A.D., just after Jesus's death.

So abundant is the testimony pointing to Christ's historical existence that Dr. F.F. Bruce, professor of biblical criticism at the University of Manchester in England, suggests that reputable historians could not possibly propagate this theory.

> "Some writers may toy with the fancy of a 'Christ myth,' but they do not do so on the ground of historical evidence. The historicity of Christ is as axiomatic for an unbiased historian as the historicity of Julius Caesar."[11]

Scott Appleby, a professor of Church History at Notre Dame, said:

> "...there is more evidence of the existence of Jesus of Nazareth than there would be for many other historical people who actually existed."

He went on to say:

> "The historical evidence of the existence of Jesus cannot be erased from any reasonable history book. There is a solid basis upon which one can intelligently believe in Jesus as a person who actually existed. Jesus cannot rationally be exposed as a myth. The Incarnation is not just a story told in Christmas carols and nativity scenes. What this means for those who will reason is that a real person from Nazareth left a sizable mark on history and started a chain of events moving far beyond his 33 years. The next question was posed by Jesus himself: 'But who do you say that I am?'"[12]

What I also find interesting is the number of religious skeptics who clearly are convinced that Jesus was a legitimate historical figure.

Will Durant, the Pulitzer Prize-winning historian who wrote the most successful work of history, the eleven-volume *The Story of Civilization,* concludes his material on Christ this way:

> "No one reading these scenes can doubt the reality of the figure behind them…"[13]

The skeptic and famed Irish historian W.E.H. Lecky says this:

> "The character of Jesus has not only been the highest pattern of virtue, but the strongest incentive in its practice, and has exerted so deep an influence, that it may be truly said that the simple record of three short years of active life has done more to regenerate and to soften mankind than all the disquisitions of philosophers and all the exhortations of moralists."[14]

Most significantly, listen to the words of the great historian H.G. Wells:

> "I am a historian, I am not a believer, but I must confess as a historian that this penniless preacher from Nazareth is irrevocably the very center of history. Jesus Christ is easily the most dominant figure in all history."[15]

Finally, this last point needs to be given strong consideration. Today the world's calendars are built around the birth of Christ. History is divided into events that took place before His birth and those that took place after His birth. This is clearly an indication of the extent to which Western culture was shaped by this man Jesus. It is quite obvious that something of universal importance began with the historical figure of Jesus. Truly, no one could have possibly invented the person of Christ.

9.3

Jesus—The Evidence

IN THE person of Christ, God has chosen not to overwhelm us or enslave us by His awesome power. If we were forced to love Him, it would not be love. At the end of the day, the big question remains: Was Jesus God incarnate?

The Bible indicates in John 1:14 that God became flesh and dwelt among us and we were able to behold His glory. In Hebrews 1:3 we learn:

> "He is the radiance of God's glory, the exact representation of God's nature."

While being tried for blasphemy, Jesus stood before the High Priest and was asked, "Are you the Christ? Are you the son of the most blessed one?" He replied, matter-of-factly, in Mark 14:62:

> "I am; and you shall see THE SON OF MAN SITTING AT THE RIGHT HAND OF POWER, and COMING WITH THE CLOUDS OF HEAVEN."

Either that statement, as incredible as it may sound, is true, or it's false. There's really no other position you can take when somebody makes a claim like that.

If it's not true, if Jesus is not God in the flesh, then what are we to make of Him? What are we to make of this historical person who led such an extraordinary life? History clearly indicates He was not a mythological figure. Was He just a great moral teacher? Was He a magician? Was He an illusionist?

On the other hand, if He was the Christ, the Messiah, the Son of God, what would that mean? It would mean quite literally everything. It would mean His entrance into the world would be the turning point in history. It would mean His teaching about life, death, and eternity would be true.

French journalist Michka Assayas had a fascinating interview with rock superstar Bono of the rock group U2. Bono is quite a popular figure and frequently is in the news. Furthermore, he is a Christian, which seems to baffle the media. In an interview, Assayas asks Bono this question:

> "Christ has His rank among the world's great thinkers. But 'Son of God'—isn't that a little far-fetched?"

Bono's response?

> "No, it's not far-fetched to me. Look, the secular response to the Christ story always goes like this. He was a prophet, obviously a very interesting guy, had a lot to say along the lines of other great prophets, be they Elijah, Mohammed, Buddha, or Confucius, but actually Christ doesn't allow you that. He doesn't let you off the hook.
>
> Christ says, 'No, I'm not saying I'm a prophet. I'm saying I am the Messiah. I am saying I am God incarnate.'
>
> And people say, 'No, no, please just be a prophet. A prophet we can take. You're a bit eccentric. We've had John the Baptist eating locusts and wild honey; we can handle that. Please don't admit to the 'M' word, the Messiah. Because, you know, we're going to have to crucify you.'
>
> And he goes, 'No, no, I know you're expecting Me to come back with an army and set you free from these creeps, but actually, I am the Messiah.'

> At this point, everyone starts staring at their shoes and says, 'Oh My God, he's going to keep saying this.'
>
> So, what you're left with in this is Christ was either Who He said He was, the Messiah, or a complete nutcase on the level of Charles Manson. I'm not joking here.
>
> The idea that the entire course of civilization for over half of the globe could have its fate changed and turned upside down by a nutcase."

And then Bono looked at the interviewer, and said,

> "For me, that's far-fetched."[16]

C.S. Lewis expressed something similar.

> "I am trying here to prevent anyone saying the really foolish thing that people often say about Him: 'I'm ready to accept Jesus as a great moral teacher, but I don't accept His claim to be God.' That is the one thing we must not say. A man who was merely a man and said the sort of things Jesus said would not be a great moral teacher. He would either be a lunatic—on a level with the man who says he is a poached egg—or else he would be the Devil of Hell. You must make your choice. Either this man was, and is, the Son of God: or else a madman, or something worse. You can shut Him up for a fool, you can spit at Him and kill Him as a demon; or you can fall at His feet and call Him Lord and God. But let us not come with any patronizing nonsense about His being a great human teacher. He has not left that open to us. He did not intend to."[17]

In another essay, Lewis says:

> "We may note in passing that He was never regarded as a mere moral teacher. He did not produce that effect on any people who actually met Him."

In other words, no one in Jesus' time would have thought to themselves, "Wow, what a wonderful teacher."

Lewis continues:

> "He produced mainly three effects. Hatred, terror, or adoration. There was no trace of people expressing mild approval."[18]

Either they hated him, they were terrorized by Him because of the unbelievable things He did, or they adored Him. They recognized Him to be God.

And then Lewis says, in conclusion, you have two choices.

> "You either have to accept or reject the story."[19]

In making decisions in life, a wise person will look at all the factors and evidence that relates to the issue and will then make a decision. Often, it is a faith decision, particularly if there is no scientific certainty to back up the choice you make. To make a decision about Jesus and His message, one must consider the historical evidence and make a determination based on the strength of the evidence. If I were to go into a court of law, I would lay out four vital points to make the case that Christ is the Son of God.

In the next few essays, I will lay out the evidence.

9.4

Jesus's Impact on History

CONSIDER HOW Jesus' simple and short life, in one of the most desolate places in the Roman Empire, had such an impact on history. Famous author, historian, and novelist H.G. Wells, who wrote the prominent book *The Outline of History* and many other books, says:

> "The historian's test of an individual's greatness is 'What did he leave to grow? Did he start men to thinking along fresh lines with vigor that persisted after him?'"[20]

What Wells is saying, in one sense, is that you can gauge the size of a ship by the size of its wake. Though Wells did not consider himself a Christian, he applied this same test to the life of Jesus by saying:

> "By this test Jesus stands first."[21]

Author Henry G. Bosch has made this observation:

> "Socrates taught for forty years, Plato for fifty, Aristotle for forty, and Jesus for only three. Yet the influence of Christ's three-year ministry infinitely transcends the impact left by the combined 130 years of teaching from these men who are

> among the greatest philosophers of all antiquity. Jesus painted no pictures, yet some of the finest painting of Raphael, Michelangelo, and Leonardo da Vinci received their inspiration from Him. Jesus wrote no poetry, but Dante, Milton, and scores of the world's greatest poets were inspired by Him. Jesus composed no music, still, Haydn, Handel, Beethoven, Bach, and Mendelssohn reached their highest perfection of melody in the hymns, symphonies, and oratories they composed in His praise. Every sphere of human greatness has been enriched by this humble carpenter of Nazareth."[22]

World-renowned historian and philosopher Will Durant wrote the classic book *The Story of Philosophy,* which is still used in many a class as an introduction to philosophy. He is a Pulitzer Prize-winning author, but he is most well-known for an eleven-volume series that he and his wife, Ariel, wrote. They spent over thirty-five years on this massive work titled *The Story of Civilization,* and the Durants were not friends of the Christian faith. In this series, one of the volumes covers the history of the Roman Empire, and from it we learn that after Jesus's death the Christian religion was considered an enemy of Rome, and this hostility lasted for over 280 years.

In 312 A.D., the edict of Milan went into law legalizing Christianity, specifically Christian worship. In 381 A.D., under Constantine, Christianity became the official religion of the Roman Empire. Durant's observation of what happened in Rome during this period of time is quite astonishing:

> "There is no greater drama in human record than the sight of a few Christians, scorned and oppressed by a succession of emperors, bearing all trials with a fierce tenacity, multiplying quietly, building order while their enemies generated chaos, fighting the sword with the Word, brutality with hope, and at last defeating the strongest state history has known. Caesar and Christ had met in the arena and Christ had won."[23]

Durant goes on to say,

> "That a few simple men should in one generation have invented so powerful and appealing a personality, so lofty an ethic and so inspiring a vision of human brotherhood would be a miracle far more incredible than any recorded in the Gospels. After two centuries of Higher Criticism the outline of the life, character, and teaching of Christ remain reasonably clear, and constitute the most fascinating feature in the history of Western man."[24]

9.5

The Resurrection

THE VERACITY of Christianity depends solely and completely on the truth or falsehood of a historical event, the Resurrection of Christ, and therefore, it needs to be determined whether it is a historical event or not. Over the years, there has been many a skeptic who understood that Christianity is falsifiable. Therefore, you would think many disbelievers would set out on a course of research to prove that Jesus did not rise from the dead.

A number of years ago, I was working on a presentation that I entitled "Jesus, Divine or Mythological?" As I was doing the research, I began to notice just how many men had set out to debunk Jesus and Christianity. Through the study of the historical record, they were convinced they could demonstrate how preposterous this claim of Resurrection really was. Yet, so many who set out on this journey, through their research, were eventually led to change their minds and become Christians.

Since I did that study, that list has grown. J.D. Anderson, Lee Strobel, William Ramsay, Josh McDowell, Frank Morison, Gilbert West—each of them exceptionally reliable as a scholar.

I think the most intriguing of all these men is Frank Morison. A very gifted English lawyer, he set out to write a book that was going to be titled *Disproving the Resurrection of Jesus.* He was convinced that he could prove what his title proclaimed. However, when he completed his research, he wrote a completely different book, now a classic, titled *Who Moved the Stone?* Morison demonstrated that the rules of evidence in a court of law confirm Jesus' Resurrection. The opening words of the book are quite powerful.

> "This study is, in some ways, so unusual and provocative that the writer thinks it desirable to state here very briefly how the book came to take its present form.
>
> In one sense, it could have taken no other, for it is essentially a confession, the inner story of a man who originally set out to write one kind of book and found himself compelled by the sheer force of circumstances to write quite another.
>
> It is not that the facts themselves altered, for they are recorded imperishably in the monuments and in the pages of human history. But, the interpretation to be put upon the facts underwent a change. Somehow the perspective shifted—not suddenly, as in a flash of insight or inspiration, but slowly, almost imperceptibly, by the very stubbornness of the facts themselves."[25]

Dallas Willard says this happens so often because, in their quest, they were forced to examine the facts and think carefully about them. As C.S. Lewis once said,

> "A young atheist can't be too careful about what he reads and must steadfastly protect his ignorance."[26]

Dr. Gary Habermas, a historian and philosopher of religion who is not only a prolific author but also considered one of the foremost experts on the Resurrection of Christ, has engineered the most comprehensive investigation ever performed on what modern scholars believe about the Resurrection. Habermas and a large team of researchers collected more than fourteen-hundred of the most scholarly words on the Resurrection written from 1975 to 2003. They included in their study only the works that were most up-to-date.

Habermas says the works they studied come from across the ideological spectrum, whether they were ultra-liberals or what he called "Bible-thumping conservatives." He and his team collected all of this research and documented only the historical facts they all could agree upon. And this is what the scholars agreed took place.

AGREEMENT ONE
Jesus died by Roman crucifixion.

AGREEMENT TWO
Jesus was buried most likely in a private tomb.

AGREEMENT THREE
Soon afterwards, the disciples were discouraged, bereaved and despondent, having lost hope.

AGREEMENT FOUR
Jesus' tomb was found empty very soon after His interment.

AGREEMENT FIVE
The disciples had experiences they believed were actual appearances of the risen Jesus.

AGREEMENT SIX
Due to these experiences, the disciples' lives were thoroughly transformed. They were even willing to die for their belief.

AGREEMENT SEVEN
The proclamation of the Resurrection took place very early from the beginning of Church history.

AGREEMENT EIGHT
The disciples' public testimony and preaching of the Resurrection took place in the city of Jerusalem, where Jesus had been crucified, and very shortly after.

AGREEMENT NINE
The Gospel message centered on the preaching of the death and Resurrection of Jesus.

AGREEMENT TEN
Sunday was the primary day for gathering and worshipping.

AGREEMENT ELEVEN
James, the brother of Jesus, and a skeptic before this time, was converted when he also saw the risen Jesus.

AGREEMENT TWELVE
Just a few years later, Saul of Tarsus, Paul, became a Christian believer due to the experience that he also believed; that he thought was an appearance of the risen Christ.[27]

As you consider this list of historical facts, number five is of particular importance.

Habermas and all of these researchers agreed that the disciples had experiences "they believed were actual appearances of the risen Jesus." Notice their research did not conclude that Jesus had risen from the dead. This is because clearly some scholars did not believe the Resurrection to be a historical fact. This is not surprising. However, all fourteen-hundred of the scholarly works did agree, at a minimum, that "the disciples had experiences they believed were actual appearances of the risen Christ."

Therefore, those who did not believe that Jesus had actually risen from the dead could only conclude that the disciples were hallucinating or they were lying. Keep this in mind as we examine agreements four and six in the list.

Historical fact number four states that Jesus' tomb was found empty. All agree there was a missing body and if Jesus did not rise from the dead then one could only conclude that someone had to have stolen the body. They also all agree in historical fact number six. The disciples' lives were thoroughly transformed, so much so they were even willing to die for their belief.

So, there's an empty tomb and the disciples' lives are transformed radically. If these are considered historical facts, how does one account for them? In relation to the empty tomb, if Jesus' body had been stolen, scholars agree you have three groups of people who would be motivated to steal it: the Romans, the Jewish authorities, or the disciples.

The problem is that the Romans and the Jewish authorities are not very plausible suspects. Once the Resurrection was being proclaimed throughout Jerusalem, all they had to do was produce the body of Christ and Christianity would have died a very quick death. As the famous British historian Arnold Toynbee said:

> "If only they could have found the body of that Jew [Jesus] Christianity crumbles into ruins."

Toynbee seemed to be frustrated that they could not find the body.

And then, you're left with the disciples. Could they have stolen the body, disposed of it, and then have spent the rest of their lives propagating a lie, particularly when the heart of their teaching was to be committed to proclaiming the truth? Does anyone seriously believe that these men who were discouraged, defeated, and who feared for their lives, would go out, steal Jesus' body, and then proceed to boldly preach the Resurrection to hostile crowds? What would motivate them to do this? Why face prison, torture, and death, all the while knowing that Jesus' dead body lay in some hidden place?

A number of years ago, there was an article in *U.S. News & World Report,* a prominent secular magazine, that was titled "Jesus' Last Days." It said, in part:

> "Yet even the most skeptical biblical scholars conceded that something extraordinary happened in Jerusalem after Good Friday to account for the radical change in the behavior

> of the disciples, who, at Jesus' arrest, had fled to their own homes in fear. Could Jesus' Resurrection account for the fact that within a few weeks they were boldly preaching their message to the very people who had sought to crush them?"[28]

Historian Thomas Arnold, author of the distinguished three-volume work *The History of Rome,* says this:

> "I have been used for many years to study the histories of other times and to examine and weigh the evidence of those who have written about them, and I know of not one fact in the history of mankind which is proved by better and fuller evidence of every sort to the understanding of a fair inquirer than the great sign God has given us that Christ died and rose again from the dead."[29]

I have concluded that these many skeptics who set out to disprove the Resurrection only to change their minds did so because they found the evidence for it to be so compelling. They could find no other explanation to account for the empty tomb, the radical change in the lives of the disciples, and the remarkable explosion of the early church—other than the fact that Jesus rose from the dead.

9.6

The Messianic Prophecies Fulfilled

IN LUKE 4:14, Luke, the physician and historian, relates to us the story of Jesus, who had been teaching in the synagogues with great wisdom. News about Him had begun to spread throughout the whole countryside. He then travels to His home in the small town of Nazareth.

It is evidently of great importance for Luke as a historian to describe the exact account of how Jesus announces His ministry. So, on a Sabbath, Jesus enters the synagogue in Nazareth and, as was the custom, stands up to read from Scriptures. It was a common Jewish practice to ask people in the synagogue to read selections from the Sacred Scripture, the Tanakh, what we know today as the Old Testament. Jesus stood, unrolled the scroll, and read from Isaiah 61.

> ". . . the spirit of the Lord God is on me because the Lord has anointed me to proclaim the good news to the poor. He has sent me to proclaim freedom for the prisoners and recovery of sight for the blind, to set the oppressed free to proclaim the year of the Lord's favor."

He then rolled up the scroll, gave it back to the attendant, and sat down.

This text that Jesus reads in Isaiah is one of the key Messianic prophecies. The Old Testament, written over a thousand-year period before Jesus was born, contains numerous references to a coming Messiah. A deliverer.

Luke continues his narrative, telling us that no one in that synagogue could take his or her eyes off of this man Jesus, who then says to the audience:

> "Today this scripture is fulfilled in your hearing."

They were perplexed and turned to each other and said, "Isn't that Joseph's son?" They weren't even sure who He was! But, of course, Jesus had lived there all of His life. Now, all of a sudden, here is Joseph's humble son declaring that He is the Messiah.

The heart of the New Testament's teaching is that Jesus is indeed the Messiah whose coming had been foretold for centuries. The problem in Jesus' day is the would-be Messiah was expected to deliver them from the bondage of Rome when, in reality, He is asserting that He came to deliver them from their sinfulness. And all of the Messianic prophecies of the Old Testament are fulfilled in the life of Jesus.

In the book of Matthew, Jesus makes a very significant statement about His life and purpose:

> "Do you think that I came to abolish the Old Testament law or the words of the prophets…I didn't come to abolish but to fulfill." (Matthew 5:17)

Again, there's that word: "fulfill." In essence, Jesus was saying that He had no intention of getting rid of Old Testament laws and instruction. He was not threatening political or social unrest and He was not going to call into question the tenets of the Jewish faith. Quite to the contrary, He had uttered the words that could have come from only the Messiah. "I came to fulfill" the words of the Old Testament prophets.

> "Remember the former things long past, for I am God and there is no other. I am God and there's no one like me... Declaring the end from the beginning and from ancient times things which have not been done, saying My purpose from a far country, truly I have spoken, truly I will bring it to pass, I have planned it, surely I will do it."
> (Isaiah 46:9)

God was revealing the fulfillment of His covenant with the Jewish nation in Sacred Scripture from the very beginning of time, telling the Jewish people exactly what was going to take place in the future. Through the prophets, He continued to let them know what they could expect with certainty. And then He tells His chosen people, in what surely must have been one of His most significant declarations, to look for the coming of the Messiah.

The coming of the Messiah is at the very heart of the Jewish faith, and, not coincidentally, it is at the very heart of the Christian faith.

Listen to these opening lines in Paul's letter to the Romans. He says,

> "Paul, a bondservant of Christ, called as an apostle, set apart for the gospel of God, which he promised beforehand. He promised beforehand through his prophets and the Holy Scriptures, concerning his son, who was born of a descendant of David according to the flesh." (Romans 1:1)

And then, again, in Luke 24, the resurrected Christ gives His final instructions to His apostles, some of the last words before His final departure:

> "These are My words which I spoke to you while I was still with you that all things which are written about Me in the Law of Moses, the prophets and the Psalms must be fulfilled."

And then, it says He opened their minds to finally understand the scriptures, saying to them:

> "Thus, it is written that the Christ will suffer and rise again from the dead the third day...You are witnesses of these things."

We see the apostle Paul on several occasions. When he would go into a new city—Acts 17, Acts 18, and Acts 19—he would go directly to the synagogue where the Jewish people were at worship. In describing it, Luke writes:

> "He would reason with them from scriptures, explaining and giving evidence that Jesus was the Christ, the Messiah."

The evidence that Paul presented to the world was powerful because of two reasons: First, there was the Resurrection, and, second, Jesus had fulfilled all the Messianic prophecies and Paul could point out these prophecies by quoting the specific verses from the Old Testament Scriptures and demonstrate how Jesus had indeed "fulfilled" them.

This helps explain the early church's explosive growth. The message was so powerful then, and that same message is valid today.

Philip Yancey says that for centuries the phrase "as predicted by the prophets" was one of the most powerful influences on people coming to faith. Justin Martyr, whom we discussed earlier, the well-known teacher and philosopher, credits his conversion to Christianity on the impression made on him by the Old Testament's predictive accuracy.[30]

French mathematician Blaise Pascal said that the fulfilled Messianic prophecies played a major role in his coming to faith. These were words he uttered over three centuries ago:

> "If a single man had written a book foretelling the time and manner of Jesus' coming, and Jesus had come in conformity

> with these prophecies, this would carry infinite weight . . . But there's much more here. There's a succession of men, over a period of four thousand years, coming consistently and invariably, one after the other, to foretell the same coming. There is an entire people proclaiming it, existing for four thousand years, to testify in a body to the certainty that they feel about it, from which they cannot be deflected by whatever threats and persecutions they may suffer. This is quite a different order of importance."[31]

And then, Peter Kreeft, the prominent philosopher at Boston College, said:

> "If you calculate the probability of any one person fulfilling, sheerly by chance, all of the Old Testament Messianic prophecies that Jesus fulfilled, it would be as astronomical as winning the lottery every day for a century. Even if Jesus deliberately tried to fulfill the prophecies, no mere man could have the power to arrange the time, place, events, and circumstances of His birth or events after His death."[32]

9.7

Lives Changed by the Messianic Prophecies

Barry Leventhal, a young Jewish man, was on top of the world back in 1966. He was the offensive captain of the UCLA football team. In the pre-season, they were predicted to finish last in the Pacific Eight Conference. However, the team stunned everyone by winning their conference championship and then went on to win the Rose Bowl. Not only was he the captain of the team, he was also the star of the Rose Bowl. This was the first Rose Bowl championship UCLA had ever won. Reflecting back on that period in his life, Leventhal recalled:

> "My life was great...I was a hero, people loved me. My Jewish fraternity chose me as the National Athlete of the Year, and I basked in the glory of it all...But soon after that victory, my very best friend, Kent, came to me and said, Barry, I've become a Christian and, as my best friend, I just wanted you to know that....I had no idea what Kent was talking about. I thought he'd always been a Christian."

However, Barry was intrigued by the change he began to notice in Kent's life. And so, several weeks later, Kent introduced Barry to a man named Hal who was a campus minister. One day they were in the student lounge and began a discussion of the issue of the Messianic prophecies. At one point the conversation grew tense as Hal was showing Barry how the predictions of the Messiah taken directly from the Old Testament had been fulfilled by Jesus. Finally, Barry blurted out:

> "How could you do this?"
>
> "Do what?" Hal asked.
>
> "Use a trick Bible," Barry charged. "You've got a trick Bible to fool the Jews."
>
> Hal responded, "What do you mean by a 'trick Bible'?"
>
> Barry said, "You Christians took those so-called Messianic predictions from your own New Testament and then rewrote them into your edition of the Old Testament in order to fool the Jews, but I guarantee you those Messianic prophecies are not in the Jewish Bible."
>
> "Now hold on, Barry. Do you happen to have a copy of the Tanakh? Do you have your own copy?"
>
> "Well, I've got one from my Bar Mitzvah. So what?"
>
> Then Hal said, "I'm going to give you some verses. I want you to write them down, and I want you to go read them in your own Tanakh and we'll just leave it at that."

The two men went back and forth, until finally Barry, wanting to get Hal off his back, agreed to check them out. Barry hurriedly wrote down the references and then got up and left. He really had no desire to meet with Hal again.

However, Barry was intrigued by their conversation, and that night found his old Tanakh that he had not opened since he was thirteen. He was shocked at what he read. Every prophecy that Hal had given him was indeed in the Tanakh. He began to think the unthinkable, what if Jesus really is the Jewish Messiah? And if He really is the Messiah, what should he do?

He decided to keep silent about this for a while and concluded that he needed to do more research, particularly if he were ever to go public with his discovery. In his study, he was most intrigued by the suffering servant described by the prophet Isaiah, in the fifty-third chapter. In Barry's own words, he says:

> "I vividly remember the first time I seriously confronted Isaiah 53, or better still, the first time it seriously confronted me," Barry explains. "Being rather confused over the identity of the servant in Isaiah 53, I went to my local rabbi and said to him, 'Rabbi, I have met some people at school who claim that the so-called Servant in Isaiah 53 is none other than Jesus of Nazareth. But I would like to know from you, who is the servant in Isaiah 53?"
>
> Barry was astonished at his response. The rabbi said, "Barry, I must admit that as I read Isaiah 53, it does seem to be talking about Jesus, but since we Jews do not believe in Jesus, it can't be speaking about Jesus."
>
> Barry didn't know a lot about formal logic at that point, but he knew enough to say to himself, that just doesn't sound kosher to me. Not only does the rabbi's so-called reasoning sound circular, it also sounds evasive and even fearful. Today Barry observes, "There are none so deaf as those who do not want to hear."
>
> "It was April now, more than three months after the glorious Rose Bowl victory, and I suddenly realized that I had nothing that withstood the test of time, let alone the test of eternity." Barry recalls. "This was most graphically demonstrated to me by the Rose Bowl victory itself. Just a few mere months after the most significant event in my life...all the glory, everything involved, was now slowly fading away into a distant memory. Is that all there is to life?"

As he continued to study, as he continued to seek, he came to the conclusion that Jesus was the Messiah. And on the afternoon of April 24, 1966, Barry knelt down by his bed, humbled himself before God, acknowledging that Jesus was the Messiah of the world and that he needed God's forgiveness that came only through the Christ. And he surrendered himself. He says:

> "There was no lightning or thunder, only God's personal presence and peace as Jesus has promised."

And since his remarkable discovery, Barry has been reaching the Jewish people with the truth that the Messiah has come. The evidence for this truth is in the Old Testament. And teaching others this evidence is the focus of Southern Evangelical seminary near Charlotte, North Carolina, where Barry currently serves as the academic dean and as a professor.[33]

One of the very fine pastors in our country today is a man by the name of Louis Lapides, a senior pastor at a church in California. He grew up in a Jewish home in Newark, New Jersey, and his family attended a conservative Jewish synagogue. When he was seventeen, his parents divorced. He recalls:

> "That really put a stake in any religious heart I may have had…On top of that, in Judaism I didn't feel as if I had a personal relationship with God. I had a lot of beautiful ceremonies and traditions, but he was the distant and detached God of Mount Sinai who said, 'Here are the rules, you live by them, you'll be okay, I'll see you later.'"

And so, Lapides became a self-styled wanderer, what we would probably call a hippie, and ended up living in Greenwich Village in the 1960s. Eventually, he was drafted and fought in the Vietnam War. He described it as a very dark period in his life.

> "I witnessed suffering. I saw body bags; I saw the devastation from war. I was extremely bothered by all the evil that I had seen."

It caused Lapides to wonder, is there a God out there to explain all this? He had survived Vietnam and had safely returned stateside; however, the only way he could deal with the trauma of his war experience was by smoking marijuana and pursuing his interest in Buddhism. In fact, he aspired to be a priest, but while studying Buddhism, he found it to be so empty. It didn't make any sense to him, so he tried Scientology, then Hinduism…It was about this time he decided to change locations. He moved to California…and one day, out on Sunset Boulevard, he encountered some Christians. He thought he would have some fun and heckle them a bit, since they were out preaching on the street to anyone who would listen. One of the Christians approached him and mentioned the name of Jesus. He tried to fend him off with his stock answer: "I'm Jewish, I can't believe in Jesus."

One of them, a pastor, spoke up:

> "Do you know the prophecies about the Messiah?"

Lapides was taken off guard.

> "Prophecies? I've never heard of them."

The minister startled Lapides by referring to some of the Old Testament predictions. Wait a minute, Lapides thought; those are my Jewish scriptures he's quoting. How could Jesus be in there? When the pastor offered him a Bible, Lapides was skeptical.

> "Is the New Testament in there?" he asked.

The pastor indicated that, yes, it was.

> "OK, I'll read the Old Testament, but I'm not going to open the other one."

Lapides was taken aback by the minister's response.

> "Fine, just read the Old Testament, and ask the God of Abraham, Isaac, and Jacob, the God of Israel, to show you if Jesus is the Messiah. Because He is your Messiah. He came to the

Jewish people initially and then He was also the Savior of the World."

To Lapides, this was all brand-new information. He'd never heard of this. It was intriguing. It was astonishing. So, he went back to his apartment, he opened the Old Testament's first book, Genesis, and he went hunting for Jesus among words that had been written hundreds of years before this carpenter of Nazareth had ever been born.

> "I was reading the Old Testament every day and seeing one prophecy after another. For instance, Deuteronomy talked about a prophet greater than Moses who will come and whom we should listen to, and I thought, 'Who can be greater than Moses?' It sounded like the Messiah. Someone as great and as respected as Moses but a greater teacher and a greater authority. I grabbed ahold of that and went searching for it… for Him."

As Lapides made his way, chapter by chapter, through the Bible, he says he was stopped cold when he read Isaiah 53. In the wake of the power of Isaiah 53, and after much time and study, he says he eventually encountered more than four dozen major prophecies in the Old Testament, which thrust him into a crucial decision.

> "I decided to open the New Testament and just read the first page . . . With trepidation, I slowly turned to Matthew as I looked up to heaven waiting for the lightning bolt to strike. Matthew's initial words leaped off the page:
>
> *'A record of the genealogy of Jesus, the son of David, the son of Abraham…' (Matthew 1:1)*
>
> Lapides' eyes widened as he recalled the moment he first read that sentence. I thought, "Wow, son of Abraham, son of David . . . It was all fitting together."

These fulfilled prophecies were very convincing to Lapides' intellect, until one day he finally concluded that Jesus was the Messiah and the New Testament Gospel message was true. Yet, it had not made its way from his head to his heart. He said not too long thereafter, he and some of his friends went out on the Mojave Desert . . . most of them with the intent to take drugs. Lapides, however, wanted to use this time for reflection. As he spent time by himself out in the desert, he made this decision, and he prayed honestly and deeply:

> "God, I've got to come to the end of this struggle. I have to know beyond a shadow of a doubt that Jesus is the Messiah. I need to know that You as the God of Israel want me to believe this."

And a while later, he says:

> "The best I can put together out of that experience is that God objectively spoke to my heart. He convinced me experientially that He exists. And at that point, out in the desert in my heart, I said, God, I accept Jesus into my life. I don't understand what I'm supposed to do with Him but I want Him. I've pretty much made a mess of my life and I need you to change me."

And he said that God began to do that in a process that continues to this day.

> "My friends knew I had changed, and they couldn't understand it. They'd say, 'Something happened to you in the desert. You don't do drugs anymore. There's something different about you.'"
>
> "I would say, 'Well, I can't explain what happened. All I know is that there is someone in my life, and it's someone who's holy, who's righteous, who's a source of positive thoughts about life, and I just feel whole.'"[34]

Today, he's a senior pastor at a large church in California.

Over the years, I have heard story after story of so many Jewish people, from all over the world, who have come to the Christian faith simply because of the convincing nature of these prophecies. You see men and women with deep intellectual and spiritual integrity who've chosen to look and seek the truth with open and honest hearts. These individuals have recognized, basically, that some of Jesus' last words to His disciples ring true.

> "Everything must be fulfilled that is written about Me in the law of Moses, the prophets, and the Psalms."

In my mind this is one of the greatest proofs that not only confirms that Jesus was the Old Testament Messiah but also validates that the Bible is the divine Word of God.

(For more on this topic, see the Appendix.)

9.8

The Power of Humility

THIS FINAL piece of evidence is quite powerful because it is so counterintuitive. Jesus did not impact the world through power, wealth, or by setting up a worldly kingdom. He did not employ any of the means that generally lead to greatness. Instead, He chose the path of humility, which was clearly by God's design.

A worldly leader who was in a position to really understand and grasp this was a man like Napoleon. Read what he said right before he died:

> "I die before my time and my body shall be given back to the earth and devoured by worms. What an abysmal gulf between my deep miseries and the eternal kingdom of Christ. I marvel that whereas the ambitious dreams of myself and of Alexander and of Caesar, should have vanished into thin air, and a Judean peasant, Jesus, should be able to stretch His hands across the centuries and control the destinies of men and nations."[35]

Think about what he is saying. Here are three famous men, Alexander the Great, Caesar, and Napoleon, seeking to control the world by power. When you see their lives contrasted with this one man Jesus, the humble carpenter, you have to marvel at how the world has been so powerfully impacted and changed through this simple life of humility. Napoleon went on to say:

> "Time the great destroyer, powerless to extinguish this sacred flame, time can neither exhaust its strength nor put a limit to its range. This is it, which strikes me most. I have often thought of it. This it is which proves to me quite convincingly the divinity of Jesus Christ."[36]

Use your imagination for a minute. If God gave you the task of creating a life, any life, for your son or your daughter, that would enable him or her to have a huge influence on the world, what would you choose? Assume you can determine their giftedness, their achievements, their wealth. What would you choose? President of the United States? King of England? Chief Justice of the Supreme Court? Senator? President of Apple? A rock star, a movie star, an Academy Award winner, Heisman trophy winner? What would you choose?

Most of us would choose for them power and influence, some type of celebrity status, a mover and a shaker, a person of substance whose character, opinions, and actions extended deeply into the world of commerce and politics.

I ask that because this is what God could have easily provided for Jesus. He could have put Him in a wealthy Roman household, or in Athens, where all the scholarly influence resided.

God could have given Jesus every advantage you would want in life, but instead, He was born and lived in the most desolate part of the Roman Empire called Palestine. He lived a very quiet life with His parents for thirty years as a carpenter. He left almost no traces of Himself on earth, and He never owned any belongings or possessions that could be enshrined in a museum. He never wrote anything. He allowed Himself to be taken into custody. He was mocked, beaten, spat upon, and then, stripped naked in front of a massive crowd. He then was taken to the cross and was crucified between two criminals for all the world to see.

And He asked God the Father to forgive those who executed Him and then was buried in a tomb. Yet somchow, Jesus and His small following have produced the dominant faith in Western civilization. How do you explain this?

Philip Yancey wrote in one of his books about the life of French philosopher and anthropologist René Girard, who was a very accomplished man. He ended his career as a distinguished professor at Stanford. At a certain point in his studies and research, Girard began to notice that a cavalcade of liberation movements—the abolition of slavery, women's suffrage, the Civil Rights movement, women's rights, minority rights, human rights—had gathered speed in the nineteenth and twentieth centuries. The trend mystified Girard because he found nothing comparable in his readings in ancient literature. Through his further research, Girard traced this phenomenon back to the historical figure of Jesus.

It struck Girard that Jesus' story cuts against the grain of every heroic story from its time. Indeed, Jesus chose poverty and disgrace. He spent his infancy as a refugee. He lived in a minority race under a harsh regime. He died as a prisoner. From the very beginning, Jesus took the side of the underdog, the poor, the oppressed, the sick, the marginalized. His crucifixion, Girard concluded, introduced a new plot to history. The victim becomes a hero by being a victim. Girard recognized that two thousand years later the reverberations from Christ's life had not stopped. And yet, ironically, at the center of the Christian faith, hangs a suffering Christ on the cross, dying in shame, for all the world to see.

And to the shock and consternation of his friends and secular colleagues, Girard announced that he had become a Christian because of the unexplainable Life of Christ.[37]

10.

Final Reflections

Most people choose to be for or against God, though many go through life not giving much thought to this eternal decision. "This same man who spends so many days and nights in rage and despair for the loss of office, or for some imaginary insult to his honor, is the very one who knows ... that he will lose all by death."

—BLAISE PASCAL

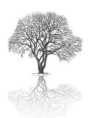

10.1

The Irrationality of Atheism

IF YOU go out to your yard or to a local park, you will notice dirt, rocks, grass, trees, plants, and maybe water in a pond or creek. Ask yourself, "How did this type of matter, gradually, over time, evolve into beings that are conscious and self-aware of themselves?" Seriously, it is inconceivable that dirt and rocks could become human beings who are "aware" and who can think and reason. In other words, matter, at some point, becomes alive and conscious. This is what the theory of evolution by natural selection is proposing.

Scientist Roy Varghese says:

> "Once you understand the nature of matter, of mass-energy, you realize that, by its very nature, it could never become 'aware,' never 'think,' never say 'I'. But the atheist position is that, at some point in the history of the universe, the impossible and the inconceivable took place. Undifferentiated matter (here we include energy), at some point became 'alive,' then conscious, then conceptually proficient, then an 'I'. Matter… has none of the properties of being conscious and given infinite time, it cannot 'acquire' such properties."[1]

The issue of "consciousness" has become a real problem for those with an atheistic worldview. Darwinian evolution has a difficult time accounting for it. As you will see, the explanation for human consciousness and thought clearly favor God.

Richard Dawkins recognizes that consciousness, thought, and human language pose a real problem. He acknowledges:

> "Neither Steve Pinker nor I can explain human subjective consciousness—what philosophers call qualia."[2]

Dawkins' friend, Harvard psychologist Steven Pinker, lays out in his book *How the Mind Works* the problem of subjective consciousness. In addressing an explanation, he is honest enough to say, "Beats the heck out of me."[3] He is acknowledging we don't really know or understand it.

Many scientists believe that the nature of consciousness is one of the biggest mysteries in life. As physicist Nick Herbert put it:

> "All we know about consciousness is that it has something to do with the head, rather than the foot."[4]

Since consciousness cannot be explained by modern science, many scientists have concluded that human consciousness is an illusion; it really does not exist. Our thoughts, reasonings, intentions, and perceptions are not real. I find this to be preposterous. For instance, Cambridge psychologist Nicholas Humphrey says:

> "Our starting assumption as scientists ought to be that on some level consciousness has to be an illusion. The reason is obvious: If nothing in the physical world can have the features that consciousness seems to have, then consciousness cannot exist as a thing in the physical world."[5]

Atheism asserts that all of life is physical and material. Therefore, your thinking is nothing more than chemical reactions in the brain. Consciousness is therefore an illusion in a world that is governed by chemical and material forces.

Dr. Francis Crick, famous for cracking the DNA code, explains it this way:

"'You,' your joys and your sorrows, your memories and your ambitions, your sense of identity and free will, are in fact no more than the behavior of a vast assembly of nerve cells and their associated molecules."

He concludes by saying:

"You're nothing but a pack of neurons."[6]

This is an incredible claim, but if there is no God, how else do you explain human consciousness? It is clearly an extreme belief. Nancy Pearcey asks a very logical question:

"Why would anyone come up with a theory so contrary to normal experience?"

She further asks:

"And why should we trust the thinking of scientists who tell us there is no such thing as thinking?"[7]

This is an example of the irrational claims of atheism. They are clinging to outlandish ideas to explain away the possibility of the existence of God.

The philosopher Galen Strawson has concluded this about the denial of consciousness:

"[It] is surely the strangest thing that has ever happened in the whole history of human thought."

He says it shows:

"...that the power of human credulity is unlimited, that the capacity of human minds to be gripped by theory, by faith, is truly unbounded. It reveals the deepest irrationality of the human mind."[8]

Dr. Daniel Wolpert is a neuroscientist and currently a neurobiology professor at Columbia University. He too is an atheist but seems to be embarrassed by the explanation his colleagues are giving for human consciousness. He has made the deliberate decision to avoid discussing the entire issue of consciousness. He says:

> "I have purposely avoided any discussion of consciousness."[9]

AS YOU are reading this book, I feel certain you recognize you have an awareness of your life, and you are actually thinking real thoughts as you are reading. If this is true wouldn't you have to conclude your consciousness is not an illusion, but an actual part of your everyday experience. So, how do you explain it?

In Antony Flew's book *There Is a God,* he reveals that one of the major influences that caused him to change his mind about atheism came from reading the book *The Wonder of the World,* by Roy Abraham Varghese. The book provides an extensive argument on the order of nature. Flew asked Varghese to write an Appendix for *There Is a God.* In the Appendix, Varghese writes:

> "Life, consciousness, mind, and the self can only come from a Source that is living, conscious, and thinking…It's simply inconceivable that any material matrix or field can generate agents who think and act. Matter cannot produce conceptions and perceptions. A force field does not plan or think. So, at the level of reason and everyday experience, we become immediately aware that the world of living, conscious, thinking beings has to originate in a living Source, a Mind."[10]

Dr. Colin McGinn is a British philosopher who has written more than twenty books and taught at a number of colleges. Best known for his work in the philosophy of the mind, he appears to be a religious skeptic who wavers over belief in God. He says:

> "We do not know how consciousness might have arisen by natural processes from antecedently existing material things."

He writes:

> "One is tempted, however reluctantly, to turn to divine assistance…It would take a supernatural magician to extract consciousness from matter."[11]

Physicist Marco Biagini has studied and written a great deal on human consciousness. He says:

> "Where does consciousness come from? The phenomenon of consciousness proves that, at a certain time, our psyche certainly began to exist in us...The laws of physics prove that consciousness cannot be the product of physical, chemical or biological processes. Therefore, the origin of our consciousness is transcendent to physical reality. We can then identify with God the necessary Cause of the existence of the psyche, being such Cause transcendent."[12]

If you will recall, back in essay 7.3, I explained how science has not been able to determine how life began on this planet. They have no explanation. Instead of giving consideration to God as an option, many have resorted to a belief that maybe alien beings somehow made their way to Earth and left certain life forms that are now our ancestors. Of course, these aliens left and never returned.

When it comes to human thought and consciousness, science has no explanation of how natural selection could generate from physical matter, something that is quite nonphysical, like consciousness. They therefore explain it away as being an illusion. It is not real. It is just a chemical reaction in your brain, that's all. Do you see why I have titled this essay "The Irrationality of Atheism"?

I think Norman Geisler provides some great insight into this:

> "If intelligent human beings can't create anything close to the human brain, why should we expect non-intelligent natural laws to do so?"[13]

I might add, that even if we could create a computer that was similar to a brain, we would all have to acknowledge that it was intelligent design that brought it into being, for only intelligence can design and create that which is intelligent. It could never happen by chance.

10.2
A Massive Contradiction

THE MAIN reason C.S. Lewis changed his mind about atheism is because he found it to be one massive contradiction. After working on this project for a number of years, I, too, have come away with a frequent observation of the contradictory nature of atheism. It is easy to claim to be an atheist; it is hard to live as if it were true. The contradiction is generally a tension between logic and life. Many atheists who have true intellectual integrity often change their minds. They recognize the contradictory nature of their atheistic worldview and, being honest people, conclude that it isn't livable.

One of the people who first spoke out about this was philosopher Friedrich Nietzsche. He saw the hypocrisy in the lives of so many atheists, and he was outraged that they did not believe in the God of the Bible yet felt an obligation to cling to Christian morality. Nietzsche strongly believed that when you abandon belief in the Christian God, you should be deprived of Christian morality. Otherwise, you are a hypocrite, or as he called it "slanderers of life." He says that all atheists should recognize that cruelty is a part of nature. He blamed Christianity for fostering the emotion of pity, which he felt was decadent. This, he believed, was consistent with natural selection and that if you were a person of integrity, you would embrace it.

The atheistic worldview has made its way into modern education. Modern educators do not adopt or support an absolute set of core values. They believe that values are purely personal and subjective and therefore should be left up to the individual. You are to establish your own values. However, those same educators are shocked when they discover that many of their students are cheating on tests.

The contradictory nature of atheism is particularly evident when someone has accepted the evolutionary premise but then tries to set up a moral framework for life.

A number of years ago a controversial book came out that explained the relationship between evolution and sexual assault. The title of the book was *The Natural History of Rape: Biological Bases of Sexual Coercion.* The two authors were college professors who made the outlandish claim that biologically speaking, rape is not a pathology. It is a behavior that has been adapted to maximize the reproductive process. It is part of the evolutionary process. The book calls rape "a natural biological phenomenon that is a product of the evolutionary heritage." They said it is akin to "the leopard's spots and the giraffe's elongated neck."

The authors were shocked by all the controversy the book caused. Their reasoning was simple logic; behavior that has survived over time must have some type of evolutionary advantage; otherwise, it would have been eliminated by natural selection.

One of the authors, Randy Thornhill, defended the book on National Public Radio (NPR). He found himself deluged by a series of enraged phone calls but reasoned that the logic is inescapable. If evolution is true, he explains:

> "Every feature of every living thing, including human beings, has an underlying evolutionary background."

And then he said:

> "That is not a debatable matter."

Apparently, he used that phrase "that is not a debatable matter" a number of times because of his belief that evolution by natural selection is a proven fact.

For those who share Mr. Thornhill's belief that evolution is a scientific fact, they have no defense against its application to human behavior. This left Mr. Thornhill's critics hamstrung because most of them accept the same evolutionary assumptions that he has accepted and, therefore, have no means to argue with his conclusion.

I read about a somewhat humorous moment in that NPR radio program. Thornhill was squaring off with a prominent feminist who had authored a book on rape titled *Against Our Wills.* As you can imagine, she was quite outspoken over his ridiculous rape theory. Thornhill responded with this insulting remark: "You are starting to sound just like the religious right."[14]

Though there is some humor in this story, the point being made is serious. Evolution and evolutionary ethics go together. This is what Nietzsche firmly believed and the point Thornhill was making. They are a package deal. He was saying if you don't like this conclusion, you should abandon your beliefs in evolution and turn to God.

EVEN RICHARD Dawkins acknowledged he cannot live with the consequences of his professed atheistic worldview. Several years ago, he was in Washington, D.C., promoting one of his books. After making a presentation, he took questions from the audience. A young man asked him:

> "If humans are machines, and it is inappropriate to blame or praise them for their actions, then should we be giving you credit for the book you are promoting?"

Dawkins clearly was taken aback and responded:

> "I can't bring myself to do that—I actually do respond in an emotional way and I blame people; I give people credit."

The young man responded:

> "But don't you see that as an inconsistency in your views?"

Dawkins' response was stunning:

> "I sort of do, yes. But it is an inconsistency that we sort of have to live with—otherwise life would be intolerable." [15]

He was admitting that, in practice, no one can truly live with an atheistic worldview; it would be intolerable.

On another occasion, back when Bill Clinton was in trouble for various sexual escapades, people were offering evolutionary explanations for his behavior. At the time, Dawkins agreed by explaining that our ancestors (the animal kingdom) were clearly not monogamous but instead harem builders. Our male ancestors, according to Dawkins, monopolized power and wealth and would sexually monopolize females in order to ensure the survival of their genes. So, in Dawkins' view, President Clinton should get a pass because his behavior is simply a reflection of his genetic past.

However, Dawkins began to get nervous for offering a genetic excuse for immorality, and he obviously did not want to give men an excuse for being philanderers. It was also at a time when he was married. So, he confided to several people that he'd made an "un-Darwinian personal decision to be deliberately monogamous." However, Dawkins believes that we are programmed by our genes through natural selection. So, how in the world does someone make an "un-Darwinian decision?" Here, again, you see the contradiction of his beliefs with how he actually lives his life.[16]

DR. EDWARD Slingerland is a distinguished scholar and professor of Asian Studies at the University of British Columbia. In his book *What Science Offers the Humanities,* he identifies himself as an unabashed atheist and materialist. He argues that Darwinian evolution leads logically to the fact that human beings are robots, and therefore your will as a person to make decisions is an illusion. Machines don't have a free will. Slingerland then turns around and admits it is an illusion that is almost impossible to shake. It is hard for us to believe that we don't have a free will to make decisions.

He also acknowledges that his view of humans as robots is contrary to ordinary experience. As he looks at his daughter, he says:

> "At an important and ineradicable level, the idea of my daughter as merely a complex robot carrying my genes into the next generation is both bizarre and repugnant to me."

Such a reductionist view "inspires in us a kind of emotional resistance and even revulsion."

He goes on to say:

> "If you do not feel that revulsion, something is wrong with you. There may well be individuals who lack this sense, and who can quite easily and thoroughly conceive of themselves and other people in purely instrumental, mechanistic terms, but we label such people 'psychopaths,' and quite rightly try to identify them and put them away somewhere to protect the rest of us."[17]

It is very difficult to live with a worldview that cannot rationally explain everyday life. It only seems logical that if your worldview does not work out in the real world, there must be something wrong with it. Nancy Pearcey says a good way to evaluate a worldview is to submit it to a very practical test: "Can we live by it?" Does it fit what we experience in life?[18]

When you examine the two worldviews we have been considering in these essays, we should ask the question suggested by Tim Keller: "Which account has the most explanatory power to make sense of what we see in the world?" Ultimately, the worldview that is true will be consistent with the real world and the one that is untrue will present a view of life that is not in harmony with reality.

The Christian worldview provides a consistent, rational way to look at life. It is not contradictory in the moral realm, and it teaches that we are made in the image of God, which gives us the basics of human dignity and human rights. It also explains how we got here and what is our purpose, which is essential in finding meaning in life. Ultimately, Christians live comfortably and consistently with their worldview because it fits the real world in which they live.

This reminds me of the great British philosopher C.E.M. Joad, who was agnostic most of his life. Later in life, he became a Christian and wrote a book on his spiritual experience titled *The Recovery of Belief*, which was published a year before he died. What was interesting is the reason he gave for this decision. He said it was a result of intellectual observation. After studying all the issues and all the evidence it became apparent to him that the Christian theistic view of life covered more of the facts of experience than any other. Therefore, he said, "I have been gradually led to embrace it."[19]

10.3

Faith Needs a Foundation

THE PRIMARY objective in writing this book was to help people see how a God-centered worldview makes sense of what we see and experience in life. I have tried to demonstrate that Christianity is logical, non-contradictory, and more fully true to the facts of human existence than atheism. It clearly leads to a more dignified and compassionate view of human life. The bottom line: It has greater explanatory power than atheism. The reason for this is because it is true. God exists. When you live in harmony with His design you will experience a coherence to your life, which will help make sense of the world.

However, it is important to understand that God has chosen not to overwhelm us in a way that would force us to believe in Him and have a relationship with Him. He desires for us to love Him but not out of overpowering fear.

The great Danish philosopher Søren Kierkegaard has given us a parable that provides great insight into how God reveals Himself to us.

It is the parable of a young king who was single and desired a queen. His palace overlooks the marketplace, and one day he sees a young peasant girl come out to do her shopping. He's quite taken by her beauty and her easy smile. He notices how kind she is to everyone and how they light up when she says hello. She walks to a food stall, buys some food and then she disappears. The king is quite taken by her, yet she has no idea that the king of this country has any idea who she is.

The next day, he looks for her and again he sees her. Before long, he looks for her every day at the same time out in the marketplace. One day, he realizes that he is hopelessly in love with this peasant girl who has no idea he has been watching her. Now, he realizes that as king, as the sovereign of this country, he could force her to marry him and be his wife and queen. Yet, he also realizes that forcing her won't really make her love him, and he would never know if she truly loved him. And so, he makes the decision to take off his crown, take off his royal clothes, and dress as a peasant, and enter her world.

God chose to send His Son, from His throne of glory, into the world as a child, to serve as God's special revelation and to demonstrate the incredible love of God.

God has given us ample evidence to believe. We are called to put our faith in Him. Faith is an easily misunderstood word. Every day we operate out of faith. We put our faith in airplanes, elevators, and doctors. In one sense, we trust them with our very lives.

Augustine, considered by many to be one of the great Christian thinkers, defined faith as "trust in a reliable source." He recognized that the source, the evidence we put our faith in, needs to be reliable and true. If you will remember in essay 5.3, I shared the words from Jean-Paul Sartre at the end of his life as he wavered in his atheistic belief. He was in despair and said he did not want to die in despair. He wanted to die with hope and faith. He then said that "…faith needs a foundation."

Sartre is right on target. Faith without a foundation is blind faith. It is blind speculation. The foundation of our faith is the evidence God has given us. It is the evidence I have laid out in these essays. The most significant evidence we have been given is the life of Jesus, God's special revelation.

I sometimes wonder how well we know ourselves, particularly the deep thoughts and intentions of the heart. I do not think we realize how feelings, desires, and emotions have such a great influence over the decisions and choices we make. They often will cause us to bypass our logic and reason, and lead us away from what is true. What I have concluded is that although our emotions and feelings may be real, they are unreliable.

As I work with people who are attempting to come to grips with the Christian faith, I often wonder what is going on in their innermost being. Are they being honest with me? Are they being honest with themselves? Are they being honest with God? Do they understand the tension that exists between the mind and the heart, and that this tension often paralyzes us and keeps us from following the truth?

One of the most wonderful examples that captures the essence of this human struggle to find Christ can be found in the life of Sheldon Vanauken. In his wonderful book *A Severe Mercy*, Vanauken details his long spiritual journey. He first describes himself as an agnostic, but then later admits he was actually an easygoing theist who regarded Christianity as a sort of fairy tale.

As I mentioned in a previous essay, Vanauken lived in different places in the world, yet he somehow struck up a long-distance friendship with C.S. Lewis. Much of the book is an exchange of letters between the two of them. In his letters, Vanauken would ask the spiritual questions that troubled him most, and Lewis would patiently and intelligently respond.

Vanauken describes the spiritual breakthrough that brought him to faith. Please take note of his thought process and how honest he is with himself:

"Christianity—in a word, the divinity of Jesus—seemed probable to me. But there is a gap between the probable and proved. How was I to cross it? If I were to stake my whole life on the Risen Christ, I wanted proof. I wanted certainty. I wanted to see him eat a bit of fish. I wanted letters of fire across the sky. I got none of these. And I continued to hang about on the edge of the gap."

At this point, he realized that he was in kind of a spiritual limbo. He described it in these words:

> "The position was not, as I had been comfortably thinking all these months, merely a question of whether I was to accept the Messiah or not. It was a question of whether I was to accept Him—or reject. My God! There was gap behind me, too. Perhaps the leap to acceptance was a horrifying gamble—but what of the leap to rejection? There might be no certainty that Christ was God—but, by God, there was no certainty that He was not. If I were to accept, I might, and probably would, face the thought through the years: 'Perhaps, after all, it's a lie; I've been had!' But, if I were to reject, I would certainly face the haunting, terrible thought: 'Perhaps it's true—and I have rejected my God!' This was not to be borne. I could not reject Jesus. There was only one thing to do, once I had seen the gap behind me. I turned away from it and flung myself over the gap toward Jesus."

A few days later, he wrote these words to C.S. Lewis:

> "I choose to believe in the Father, Son, and Holy Ghost—in Christ, my Lord and my God. Christianity has the ring, the feel of unique truth. Of essential truth. By it, life is made full instead of empty, meaningful instead of meaningless. Cosmos becomes beautiful at the Centre, instead of chillingly ugly beneath the lovely pathos of spring. But the emptiness, the meaninglessness, and the ugliness can only be seen, I think, when one has glimpsed the fullness, the meaning, and the beauty. It is when heaven and hell have both been glimpsed that going back is impossible. But to go on seemed impossible, also. A glimpse is not a vision. A choice was necessary: and there is no certainty. One can only choose a side. So I—I now choose my side."[20]

The words of Vanauken that seem to be so pivotal are "A choice is necessary." He is correct. A choice has to be made.

I learned the truth of this because you cannot remain neutral toward Jesus. To not make a decision, in the end, is to make the decision not to accept Him. At a certain point in Jesus' ministry, He confronted His own disciples with the necessity of a choice. In the sixth chapter of John (vs. 66-69), many of His followers began to withdraw from Him and chose to no longer follow Him. They did not like what He was teaching. He is standing there, with only the twelve disciples remaining. He asks them, "Do you not want to leave too and go with them?" Peter responds and says:

"Lord, to whom shall we go? You have words of eternal life. We have believed and have come to know that You are the Holy One of God."

What a powerful response by Peter. If we do not put our faith in You, Jesus, whom will we look to for eternal life? Whom will we put our hope and faith in? This is the question we are all confronted with. It is the choice we have to make. If I do not look to Christ for eternal life, to whom shall I look? Whom will I rely upon? Remember, faith must have a foundation, and if Jesus is not that foundation, who or what will be?

It is a choice that only you can make.

Afterwords: Making a Choice

WHEN I look at my life and my own spiritual journey, in many ways I was just like so many people. The great barrier that kept me from coming to faith was pride. Though I had always believed the Christian message to be true, I chose to live intentionally without God in my life. The simple reason is that I loved the approval of man more than I loved the approval of God. I was like Pascal's friends who had no interest in spiritual truth because they feared the opinion of their friends and dreaded being labeled weak and religious. I, too, desired to court the favor of the worldly, popular, and successful people in my sphere of influence. I had an image to keep up and an audience to impress.

Though life was good, something began to happen in me that was totally unexpected and completely out of my control. I began to experience an emptiness in my life that I could not understand. Over time, I concluded that maybe I should start going to church, hoping that the emptiness would disappear, but it didn't.

So, I began what I would call a spiritual search, reading books and the Bible. I still believed the Christian message to be true, but I had hoped there was a way for me to be a Christian on my own terms. To be quite honest, I was afraid to become a Christian. I was afraid of how God would change my life and what people would think of me if I became a serious follower of Jesus. Yet the sense of an empty, meaningless life persisted.

Then through a series of circumstances, particularly when one of my closest friends was involved in a serious motorcycle accident, I came to a startling conclusion. A choice had to be made. I could not remain neutral toward Jesus. In fact, Christ Himself said, "You are either with Me or against Me." There is no middle ground.

As I recall, what caused me to wave the white flag and surrender was when I finally asked myself, "What is the alternative?" The alternative was to reject Christ's offer of the forgiveness of my sins, to reject His offer of eternal life, and to walk through life alone without Him. I could not reject Him. Therefore, one evening, I made the decision to humble myself, surrender to Christ, and put my faith in Him. All I can say is that since that day, my life has not been the same. Walking through life with Christ has been the ultimate adventure, and I never dreamed that my life with Him as my guide would have turned out so well.

Endnotes

INTRODUCTION

1. Sam Harris, *Letter to a Christian Nation* (United Kingdom: Alfred A. Knopf, 2006), 5.
2. Armand Nicholi, *The Question of God: C.S. Lewis and Sigmund Freud Debate God, Love, Sex, and the Meaning of Life* (New York: Free Press, 2002), 8.
3. Nicholi, *The Question of God,* 9.

SECTION 1

Essay 1.1

4. Ravi Zacharias, *A Shattered Visage: The Real Face of Atheism* (Grand Rapids: Baker Books, 1990), 12.
5. Nicholi, *The Question of God,* 7–8.
6. Albert M. Wolters, *Creation Regained: Biblical Basics for a Reformational Worldview* (Grand Rapids, MI: Eerdmans, 1985), 4.
7. Nicholi, *The Question of God,* 7–9.
8. "Knowing God," in *The Tim Keller Sermon Archive.* New York City: Redeemer Presbyterian Church. Exported from Logos Bible Software, 12:49 PM June 2, 2020.
9. *Richard Dawkins vs. John Lennox: The God Delusion Debate*, University of Alabama at Birmingham, October 3, 2007 (Birmingham: New Day Entertainment, 2007), DVD.

Essay 1.2

10. Francisco Uribe, "Believing Without Evidence is Always Wrong," Aeon, November 5, 2018, https://aeon.co/ideas/believing-without-evidence-is-always-morally-wrong
11. Samuel Leith, *The Impossibility of Agnosticism* (London: Inter-Fellowship Press, 1950).
12. Francis Collins, "The Language of God: A Scientist Presents Evidence for Belief" in *A Place for Truth: Leading Thinkers Explore Life's Hardest Questions,* ed. Dallas Willard. (Downers Grove: InterVarsity Press, 2010), 77.
13. Francis Collins, "From Atheism to Belief" in *Mere Christians: Inspiring Stories of Encounters with C.S. Lewis,* ed. Mary Anne Phemister, Andrew Lazo. (Grand Rapids: Baker Books, 2009), 79.
14. Jill Carattini, "A Reasonable Faith," in *A Slice of Infinity, RZIM,* October 26, 2006, //www.rzim.org/listen/just-a-thought/a-reasonable-faith-2.

Essay 1.3

15. Douglas Groothuis, *Truth Decay: Defending Christianity Against the Challenges of Postmodernism* (Downers Grove: InterVarsity Press, 2000), 9.
16. Antony Flew, *There is a God: How the World's Most Notorious Atheist Changed His Mind* (New York: HarperOne, 2007), 88.
17. Frank Turek, *Stealing From God: Why Atheists Need God to Make Their Case* (Colorado Springs: NavPress, 2014), 73.
18. Nicholi, *The Question of God,* 86.
19. Ibid., 87.

SECTION 2

Essay 2.1

1. Ravi Zacharias, *Deliver Us From Evil & Jesus Among Other Gods* (Nashville: Thomas Nelson, 1997), 148.
2. Nancy Pearcey, *Finding Truth: Liberating Christianity from Its Cultural Captivity* (Wheaton: Crossway Books, 2004), 141-142.
3. Greg Koukl, *Tactics: A Game Plan For Discussing Your Christian Convictions* (Grand Rapids: Zondervan, 2009), 136-137.
4. Nancy Pearcey, *Saving Leonardo: A Call To Resist The Secular Assault On Mind, Morals, & Meaning* (Nashville: B&H Publishing Group, 2010), 42.
5. Tim Keller, *The Reason for God: Belief In An Age Of Skepticism* (New York: Penguin Books, 2008), 26.

6. Andrew Delbanco, *The Death of Satan: How Americans Have Lost the Sense of Evil* (United States: Farrar, Straus, and Giroux, 1996), 3.
7. Alvin Plantinga, *The Analytic Theist* (United Kingdom: W.B. Eerdmans Publishing Company, 1998), 339.
8. Keller, *The Reason for God,* 27.

Essay 2.2

9. Darrow, Clarence. "Attorney Clarence Darrow's Plea for Mercy in the Franks Case and Prosecutor Robert E. Crowe's Demand for the Death Penalty in the Loeb-Leopold Case" (Chicago, IL: Wilson Publishing Company, 1924), 5-85.
10. Translated by Norman Cameron and R. H. Stevens. *Hitler's Table Talk 1941–44* (London: Weidenfeld and Nicolson, 1973. First published in 1953), 51.
11. Michael Burleigh, *Death and Deliverance: 'Euthanasia' in Germany 1900-1945* (Cambridge: Cambridge University Press, 1994), 188.
12. John Warwick Montgomery, "Why Human Rights Are Impossible Without Religion," in *A Place for Truth* (Downers Grove: InterVarsity Press, 2010), 264–266.

Essay 2.3

13. Burrhus Frederic Skinner, *Beyond Freedom and Dignity* (United Kingdom: Knopf), 1971.
14. David Gelertner, *Time Magazine,* "How Hard is Chess?" June 24, 2001.
15. Fred Barnes, "Politics," *Vogue Magazine,* September 1989, 542.
16. Rodney Allen Brooks, *Flesh and Machines: How Robots Will Change Us* (United States: Vintage Books, 2003), 174.
17. Charles Darwin, *The Origin of Species by Means of Natural Selection: Or the Preservation of Favoured Races in the Struggle for Life* (Italy: Penguin Books Limited, 1982).
18. Viktor E. Frankl, *The Doctor and the Soul: From Psychotherapy to Logotherapy* (United Kingdom: Knopf Doubleday Publishing Group, 2010), xxvii.
19. Alister McGrath, *If I Had Lunch with C.S. Lewis: Exploring the Ideas of C.S. Lewis On the Meaning of Life* (Colorado Springs: Tyndale, 2014), 147–148.
20. Herbert George Wells, *Mind at the End of Its Tether* (United Kingdom: W. Heinemann, 1945).
21. Os Guinness, *Time for Truth: Living Free in a World of Lies, Hype and Spin* (Grand Rapids: Baker Books, 2000), 102–103.

22. Tim Keller, "Reason for God" in *A Place for Truth: Leading Thinkers Explore Life's Hardest Questions,* ed. Dallas Willard. (Downers Grove: InterVarsity Press, 2010), 67.

Essay 2.4

23. Mortimer Adler, *The Difference of Man and the Difference it Makes* (New York: Fordham University Press, 1993), 283.
24. Philip Yancey, "Dachau—and a Pastoral Call," *Christianity Today,* January 13, 1989.

Essay 2.5

25. Steve Inskeep, heard on "Morning Edition," NPR, October 4, 2017.
26. Moreland, J.P., presentation at Rice University at a Veritas Forum.
27. Steve Turner, "The Creed," from *Can Man Live Without God* (Nashville: Word Publishing, 1994) by Ravi Zacharias, 42.

Essay 2.6

28. Ron Carlson, *Fast Facts on False Teachings* (Eugene: Harvest House Publishing, 1994), 28, 29.
29. Alvin Schmidt, H*ow Christianity Changed the World* (Grand Rapids: Zondervan, 2004), 48, 122, 147, 166, 289.
30. Yancey, *Vanishing Grace,* 167–169.
31. Paul Chamberlain, https://taneabirsa.wordpress.com/2017/06/06/as-an-atheist-i-truly-believe-africa-needs-god-by-paul-chamberlain

Essay 2.7

32. Philip Yancey, *Where is God When It Hurts: A Comforting, Healing Guide for Coping With Hard Times* (Grand Rapids: Zondervan Publishing, 1990), Preface.
33. Tim Keller, *Walking with God Through Pain and Suffering* (New York City: Penguin Group, 2013), 5.
34. C.S. Lewis, *The Problem of Pain: How Human Suffering Raises Almost Intolerable Intellectual Problems* (Stuttgart, Germany: MacMillan Publishing, 1962), 93.
35. Debate between Bart Ehrman and Dinesh D'Souza on the issue of Pain and Suffering at The University of North Carolina, October 8, 2009.
36. Philip Jenkins, *The Next Christendom: The Coming of Global Christianity,* United States: Oxford University Press. Revised and Updated edition, March 31, 2002), 220.

37. Keller, *Walking With God Through Pain and Suffering,* 106, 107.

Essay 2.8

38. Yancey, *Where Is God When It Hurts,* 55, 56.
39. Ibid., 85-87.
40. Ernest Gordon, *Through the Valley of the Kwai* (New York City: Harper & Row, 1962).

SECTION 3

Essay 3.1

1. Richard Dawkins, *River Out of Eden: A Darwinian View of Life* (New York City: Basis Books, 1992), 133.
2. Justin Brierly Interview posted on www.premierchristianradio.com. July 1, 2014.
3. Turek, *Stealing from God*, 92.
4. Ravi Zacharias, *Can Man Live Without God* (Nashville: Word Publishing, 1994), 20.
5. Tim Keller, *Making Sense of God: An Invitation to the Skeptical* (New York City: Penguin Group, 2016), 47.
6. Tim Keller, Sermon at Redeemer Presbyterian, "Wisdom: Strangeness and The Order of God," October 30, 2004.

Essay 3.2

7. Philip Yancey, *What Good is God: In Search Of A Faith That Matters* (New York: FaithWords, 2010), 60.
8. Byron Johnson, *More God, Less Crime: Why Faith Matters and How It Could Matter More* (Ukraine: Templeton Press, 2011).
9. Yancey, *Vanishing Grace,* 159, 160.
10. Debate at Oxford University, March 3, 1993 included in the publication "Ultimate Issues Vol. 9 No. 1."
11. "Chicago Sun Times," August 24, 1975, Section 1B, p.8.
12. Lord Acton—Chuck Colson in *Breakpoint Magazine* "The Power of Religion," October 4, 1993.
13. Guenter Lewy, *Why America Needs Religion: Secular Modernity and Its Discontents,* (Grand Rapids, MI: Eerdmans Publishing, 1996).

Essay 3.3

14. Turek, *Stealing from God,* 101.
15. Donald Miller, *Blue Like Jazz* (Nashville: Thomas Nelson, 2003), 22.
16. George Mavrodes, "Religion and the Queerness of Morality," in Robert Audi and William Wainwright, *Rationality, Religious Belief, and Moral Commitment* (Ithaca, NY: Cornell University Press, 1986), 213–26.
17. Keller, *Making Sense of God,* 191.
18. Philip Yancey, *Soul Survivor* (New York City: Doubleday, 2001), 115, 116.
19. Peter Kreeft, *C. S. Lewis for the 3rd Millennium: Six Essays on the Abolition of Man* (San Francisco: Ignatius Press, 1994), 91.

Essay 3.4

20. Ravi Zacharias, *Light in the Shadow of Jihad: The Struggle for Truth* (New York City: Multnomah Publishers, 2002), 24.
21. Albert Einstein, "Science and God: A Dialogue" in *Forum and Century 83* (June 1930).
22. James Davidson Hunter and Paul Nedelisky, *Science and the Good: The Tragic Quest for the Foundation of Morality* (New Haven: Yale University Press, 2018), 11.
23. Ibid., 156, 157.
24. Ibid., 199.

Essay 3.5

25. G.K. Chesterton, "The New Rebel" from Orthodoxy (UK: John Lane Company, 1908).
26. Norman Geisler, *Intellectuals Speak Out About God* (Chicago: Regnery Gateway, 1984), 147, 148.
27. Francis Schaeffer, *How Should We Then Live: The Rise and Decline of Western Thought and Culture (*Old Tappan: Fleming H Revell Co., 1976), 178–181.

SECTION 4

Essay 4.1

1. Richard Dawkins, *River Out of Eden: A Darwinian View of Life* (New York City: Harper Collins, 1995), 132, 133.

2. David Friend, "The Meaning of Life," *Life Magazine,* 1991.
3. David Benatar, *The Human Predicament: A Candid Guide to Life's Biggest Questions.* (United States: Oxford University Press, 2017), 201.
4. "Interview with Woody Allen," *Esquire Magazine,* May 1977.
5. Woody Allen Interview, "Woody Allen: Still Working, Still Terrified," in *Newsweek Magazine* by Jennie Yabroff, August 7, 2008.

Essay 4.2

6. Howard Kushner wrote this in the forward of Victor Frankl's *Man's Search for Meaning 2006 Edition.*
7. Yancey, *Vanishing Grace,* 32.

Essay 4.3

8. Kelly Kullberg, *Finding God Beyond Harvard* (Downers Grove: InterVarsity Press, 2006), 93, 94.

Essay 4.4

9. John O'Neil, *The Paradox of Success* (New York City: Penguin, Putman, Inc., 1994), 177.

Essay 4.5

10. Speech by Billy Graham at The National Prayer Breakfast in Washington D.C., February 1993.
11. Kullberg, *Finding God Beyond Harvard,* 26, 27.
12. Katherine Kaplan, "College Faces Mental Health Crisis" from *The Harvard Crimson,* January 12, 2004.
13. *The Stanford Encyclopedia of Philosophy,* Section on Albert Camus, October 27, 2011.
14. Thomas Masaryk, *Suicide and the Meaning of Civilization*, Chapter 5, (Chicago: University of Chicago Press, 1970).

Essay 4.6

15. Wikipedia: "Life of Albert Camus."
16. Howard Mumma, *Albert Camus and the Minister* (Brewster: Paraclete Press, 2000), 86, 87.
17. Ibid., 89.
18. Ibid., 95.

SECTION 5

Essay 5.1

1. Victor Frankl and William Winslade, *Man's Search for Meaning* (Boston: Beacon Press, 1959), 37.
2. Donald McCullough, *Waking From the American Dream* (Downers Grove: Intervarsity Press, 1988), 102.
3. Francis Crick. *Astonishing Hypothesis: The Scientific Search for the Soul* (United Kingdom: Scribner, 1995), 3.
4. C.S. Lewis, *On Living in an Atomic Age In Present Concerns* (San Diego: Harcourt Books, 2002), 76.
5. Nancy Pearcey, *Total Truth,* (Wheaton: Crossway Books, 2004), 317, 318.
6. Francis August Schaeffer, *The God who is There: Speaking Historic Christianity Into the Twentieth Century* (United Kingdom: Hodder and Stoughton, 1970), 40.
7. Susan Schaeffer MacCaulay, *How to be Your Own Selfish Pig* (Lynnfield: Chariot Books, 1982), 81–83.
8. Charles Colson, "When Atheists Believe," *Christianity Today,* October, 2009, 58.
9. Nancy Pearcey, Speech at Ohio State at Veritas Forum Seminar.

Essay 5.2

10. Alister McGrath, *Mere Apologetics* (Grand Rapids: Baker Books, 2012), 114.
11. David Robertson, *The Dawkins Letters: Revised Edition—Challenging Atheist Myths (Fern,* Scotland: Christian Focus Publications, 2010).
12. C.S. Lewis, *Surprised by Joy: The Shape of My Early Life* (New Haven: Yale University Press, 2011), 74.
13. C.S. Lewis, *On Living in an Atomic Age In Present Concerns* (San Diego: Harcourt Books, 2002), 76.
14. Pearcey, *Saving Leonardo,* 156.
15. Charles Darwin, *The Autobiography of Charles Darwin* (Perth, Australia: Serenity Press, 2008), 80, 81.

Essay 5.3

16. Tim Keller, Sermon, "Death and the Christian Hope," April 4, 2004, at Redeemer Presbyterian Church in New York City.
17. Ernest Jones, *The Life and Work of Sigmund Freud* (Germany: Basic Books, 1953), 279.

18. John Myers, *Voices from the Edge of Eternity* (Copenhagen, Denmark: Spine Books, 1971), 22, 23.
19. Donald Coggan, *The Heart of the Christian Faith* (New York City: HarperCollins, 1986), 51.
20. Svetlana Stalin, *Encyclopedia of 7,700 Illustrations,* as quoted in "Newsweek Magazine" (Rockville: Assurance Publishers, 1979).
21. Jean-Paul Sartre and Benny Levy, translated by Adrian Van Den Hoven. *Hope Now: The 1980 Interviews* (Chicago: The University of Chicago Press, 1996), 110.
22. Sumit Paul, *The Milli Gazette,* "Why Did Jean-Paul Sartre Turn to Belief Prior to Death", June 20, 2018.
23. De Marco and Wiker, *Architects of the Culture of Death,* 85.
24. Nicholi, *The Question of God,* 216.
25. James Henry Potts, *The Golden Dawn: Or Light on the Great Future: in this Life, Through the Dark Valley, and in the Life Eternal, as Seen in the Best Thoughts of Over Three Hundred Leading Authors and Scholars* (Charleston: Nabu Press, 2012), 183.

Essay 5.4

26. Nancy Pearcey, *Salvo Magazine,* Issue #44, "Silicon Debauchery," Spring 2018.
27. Fyodor Dostoyevsky, *The Brothers Karamazov* (United States: Macmillan, 1922), 704.
28. Tim Keller, Selected Sermons: "Lust; The Case of Joseph," March 12, 1995; "Love and Lust," May 6, 2012; and "Sex and the Romantic Solution," May 8, 2014.
29. Dr. Gail Bolan, "110 Million S.T.D. Infections," *The New York Times, October 2, 2017.*
30. Kirk Johnson, Lauren Noyes and Robert Rector, "Sexually Active Teenagers Are More Likely to Be Depressed and to Attempt Suicide," *The Heritage Foundation, J*une 3, 2003.
31. J. D. Graear, Sermon, "The Hebrew Delight" and podcast audio, *Still Standing,* September 6, 2009.
32. Dr. David Ley, "Open Marriage, Healthy Marriage?" *Psychology Today, January 4, 2011.*
33. J.D. Graear, "The Hebrew Delight" and *Still Standing,* September 6, 2009.
34. Lauren Winner, *Real Sex* (Grand Rapids: Brazos Press, 2005), 62.
35. Philip Yancey, *Finding God in Unexpected Places* (New York City: Doubleday, 1995), 17, 18.

36. Ibid., 19.

Essay 5.5

37. David Shimmer, "Yale's Most Popular Class Ever," *The New York Times,* January 26, 2018.
38. John Gray, *Straw Dogs* (New York: Farrar, Straus, and Giroux, 2003), 142.
39. Nicholi, *The Question of God,* 125.
40. Ibid., 123, 124.
41. Ibid., 100.
42. Ibid., 107–109.
43. Ibid., 104, 105.

SECTION 6

Essay 6.1

1. Sigmund Freud, James Strachey, Peter Gay. *The Future of An Illusion.* (United Kingdom: Norton, 1964), 42.
2. Dinesh D'Souza, *What is So Great About Christianity?* (Wheaton: Tyndale House Publishing, 2007), 266.
3. Ibid., 268.

Essay 6.2

4. "Father John", Winning essay in the John Templeton Foundation Power of Purpose Contest, 2004.
5. Mortimer Jerome Adler, *Philosopher at Large: An Intellectual Autobiography* (Kiribati: Macmillan, 1977), 39.
6. Aldous Huxley, *Ends and Means* (New Brunswick: Transaction Publishing, 2012), 310.
7. Kreeft, *C.S. Lewis for the 3rd Millennium,* 44.
8. M. Scott Peck, *People of the Lie* (United States: Touchstone, 1983), 167–168.

Essay 6.3

9. Joe Morganstern, Film Review "That's Enron-tainment," *The Wall Street Journal,* April 29, 2005.
10. "Investors Guide" *Fortune Magazine,* April 29, 2005.

Essay 6.4

11. Robert Jastrow, *God and the Astronomers* (New York City: W.W. Norton & Co., 2000), 16.
12. Hugh Ross, *Creator and the Cosmos* (Colorado Springs: NavPress, 1993), 57.
13. Fred Heeren, *Show Me God* (Miamitown: Daystar, 2000), 135.
14. Thomas Kuhn, *The Structure of Scientific Revolutions*, (Chicago: University of Chicago Press, 1970), 150.
15. Herbert Schlossberg, *Idols for Destruction* (Nashville: Thomas Nelson Publishers, 1983), 145.
16. David Brooks, "The Mental Virtues," *The New York Times.* August 29, 2014.

Essay 6.5

17. Andrew de Mello, *The Way to Love* (New York City: Doubleday, 1991), 64.
18. Paul Vitz, From a speech at the Veritas Forum at The University of Florida, 1995.
19. Lee Strobel, *The Case for Faith* (Grand Rapids: Zondervan, 2000), 234, 235.
20. David Brooks, *The Second Mountain* (New York City: Random House, 2019), 197.

Essay 6.6

21. Paul Vitz, From a speech at the Veritas Forum at The University of Florida, 1995.
22. Paul Vitz, *Faith of the Fatherless* (San Francisco: Ignatius Press, 1999), 29.
23. Ibid., 30.
24. Ibid., 50–69.
25. Ibid., 79–84.
26. Ibid., 135–137.
27. Ibid., 154–156.

SECTION 7

Essay 7.1

1. Lee Strobel, *The Case for a Creator* (Grand Rapids: Zondervan, 2004), 74.

2. Francis Collins, "The Language of God," from *A Place for Truth.* (Downers Grove: Intervarsity Press, 2010), 89.
3. David Masci, Senior Researcher, The Pew Forum, "Scientists Not Entirely Without Belief in God," from *The Los Angeles Times* and in *The Birmingham News,* November 27, 2009.
4. Joe Boot, Essay: "Dinosaurs and Digital Phones" April 19, 2007.
5. Ibid.

Essay 7.2

6. Rice Brooks, *God's Not Dead (*Nashville: Thomas Nelson, Inc. 2013), 67, 68.
7. Robert Jastrow, *God and the Astronomers* (New York City: Norton and Norton, 1992), 9.
8. Brooks, *God's Not Dead,* 69.
9. Arthur Eddington, *The Expanding Universe* (New York: MacMillan, 1933), 124.
10. Strobel, *The Case for a Creator,* 69–71.
11. Ibid., 77.
12. Ibid., 77.
13. Stephen Hawking and Roger Penrose, *The Nature of Space and Time: The Isaac Newton Institute Series of Lectures* (Princeton: Princeton University Press, 1996), 20.
14. Francis Collins, *The Language of God* (New York City: Free Press, 2006), 75
15. Stephen Hawking, *A Brief History of Time: The Updated and Expanded Tenth Anniversary Edition* (New York: Bantam, 1996), 49.

Essay 7.3

16. Strobel, *The Case for a Creator,* 19, 37, 38.
17. Strobel, *The Case for Faith,* 96.
18. J. Horgan, "In the beginning…" *Scientific American,* February 1991, 117.
19. Klaus Dose, "The Origin of Life: More Questions Than Answers", Interdisciplinary Science Reviews, Volume 13, 1988 - Issue 4, Published Online: 18 Jul 2013, 348.
20. Francis Crick, *Life Itself: Its Origin and Nature,* (New York: Simon and Schuster, 1981), 153.
21. Ibid., 88.
22. Allan Rex Sandage, as quoted in "Sizing Up the Cosmos: An Astronomer's Quest", *The New York Times,* John Noble Wilford, 12

March 1991, B9. https://www.nytimes.com/1991/03/12/science/sizing-up-the-cosmos-an-astronomer-s-quest.html

23. Charles Darwin, *On the Origin of Species* (Mineola: Dover Thrift, 2006), 119.
24. Andrew Parker, *The Genesis Enigma: Why the First Book of the Bible Is Scientifically Accurate* (United States: Penguin Publishing Group, 2009).

Essay 7.4

25. Collision: Debate, Christopher Hitchens vs. Douglas Wilson, directed by Darren Doane, 2009.
26. Yancey, *Vanishing Grace,* 179.
27. Paul Davies, Charles William. T*he Cosmic Blueprint: Order and Complexity at the Edge of Chaos* (United Kingdom: Penguin, 1995).
28. Mark Clark, The Problem of God (Grand Rapids: Zondervan, 2017), 58.
29. Ibid., 58.
30. Stephen Hawking, *A Brief History of Time* (New York City: Bantam Books, 1996), 126, 129.
31. Fred Hoyle, "The Universe: Past and Present Reflections," *Engineering and Science Magazine,* November 1981, 12.
32. Del Ratzsch, "Teleological Arguments for God's Existence," *The Stanford Encyclopedia of Philosophy,* edited by Edward N. Zalta, Winter 2009 Edition, plato.stanford.edu/archivs/win2009/entries/ technological-arguments. Accessed September 11, 2016.
33. Francis Crick, *What Mad Pursuit: A Personal View of Scientific Discovery* (New York City: Basic Books, 1988), 138.
34. *Expelled: No Intelligence Allowed.* Directed by Nathan Frankowski, Premise Media Corporation & Rampant Films, 2008.
35. Vince Vitale and Ravi Zacharias, *Jesus Among Secular Gods: The Countercultural Claims of Christ* (New York City: Faith Words, 2017), 85.
36. John J. Pasquini, A*theist Persona: Causes and Consequences* (Lanham: University Press of America, 2014), 96.
37. Thomas Nagel, *The Last Word* (Oxford: Oxford University Press, 1997), 130.
38. Vitale and Zacharias, *Jesus Among Secular Gods,* 85.

Essay 7.5

39. Pearcey, *Total Truth,* 316.
40. Speech by Francis Collins, "The Language of God," The Veritas

Forum at California Institute of Technology, 2009.
41. Steven Weinberg, *Facing Up: Science and Its Cultural Adversaries* (Cambridge: Harvard University Press, 2001), 45-46.
42. Paul Davies, *God and the New Physics* (New York: Simon & Schuster, 1983) 189.
43. Alexander Tsiaras, *"Conception to Birth—Visualized." TED: Ideas Worth Spreading,* December 2010. https://www.ted.com/talks/alexander_tsiaras_conception_to_birth_visualized
44. Albert Einstein, Freeman Dyson. *The Ultimate Quotable Einstein* (United States: Princeton University Press, 2019), 161.

SECTION 8

Essay 8.1

1. James Agresti, "A Scientific Dissent from Darwinism," Center for Science and Culture, Updated October 2007. https:/www.dissentfromdarwin.org.
2. Robert B. Laughlin, *A Different Universe: Reinventing Physics from the Bottom Down* (New York City: Basic Books, 2005), 168, 169.
3. Charles Darwin, *Origin of Species* (New York City: Dover Thrift, 2006), 119.
4. Hugh Ross, In a personal interview with Rice Brooks, October 26, 2012.

Essay 8.2

5. Brouwer, A., "General Paleontology," [1959], Transl. Kaye R.H., Oliver & Boyd: Edinburgh & London, 1967, 162–163.
6. Lee Strobel. *The Case for Faith.* (Grand Rapids: Zondervan, 2000), 91.
7. James D. Agresti, *Rational Conclusions* (United States: Documentary Press, 2009), 260.
8. Ibid., 289.
9. Ibid., 289.
10. Luther Sutherland, *Darwin's Dilemma: Fossils and Other Problems* (Green Forest: Master Books, 1984), 89.
11. David Pilbeam, "Rearranging Our Family Tree," *Human Nature,* June 1978, 44.
12. D.V. Ager, "The Nature of the Fossil Record," *Proceedings of the Geological Association,* vol. 87, No. 2 (1976), pp. 132–3.
13. Luther D. Sunderland, *Darwin's Enigma: Fossils and Other Problems*

(United States: Master Book Publishers, 1984), 88.
14. Niles Eldredge. *Timeframes: The Rethinking of Darwinian Evolution and the Theory of Punctuated Equilibria* (New York: Simon and Schuster, 1985), 44.
15. Richard E. Simmons III, *Reliable Truth* (Birmingham: Union Hill Publishing, 2013), 84-85.

Essay 8.3

16. Strobel, *The Case for a Creator,* 61, 62.
17. Henry Gee, *In Search of Deep Time: Beyond the Fossil Record to a New History of Life* (New York City: The Free Press, 1999).
18. Bolton Davidheiser, *Evolution and the Christian Faith* (Birmingham: Presbyterian and Reformed Publishing Company, 1971), 326.
19. Blanchard, *Has Science Got Rid of God?,* 59, 60.
20. Brian Switek, "Bones that Tell a Tale," *The Wall Street Journal,* October 8, 2011, C6.

Essay 8.4

21. J.P. Moreland and Muehlhoff, *The God Conversation* (Downers Grove: Intervarsity Press, 2007), 132.
22. Charles Darwin, *The Life and Letters of Charles Darwin,* (London: John Murray, 1988), 2:273.
23. Claudia Wallis, "The Evolution Wars," *Time Magazine,* August 7, 2005, 30.
24. Blanchard, *Has Science Got Rid of God?,* 66.
25. Brooks, *God's Not Dead,* 105, 106.
26. Ibid., 219, 221.

Essay 8.5

27. Candace Adams, "Leading Nanoscientist Builds Big Faith," *Baptist Standard,* March 15, 2000.

Essay 8.6

28. Pearcey, *Finding Truth,* 177–181.

Essay 8.7

29. Richard Lewontin, "Billions and Billions of Demons," *The New York Review of Books,* January 9, 1997, p.31.
30. David Berlinski, *The Devil's Delusion: Atheism and Its Scientific Pretensions*

(United States: Crown Forum, 2008), 112.
31. Richard Dawkins, *The Blind Watchmaker* (New York City: W.W. Norton, 1986), 287.
32. Rodney Stark, *For The Glory of God: How Monotheism Led to Reformations, Science, Witch-Hunts and the End of Slavery* (Princeton: Princeton University Press, 2003), 176.
33. Ibid., 184.

SECTION 9

Essay 9.1

1. Gilbert Keith Chesterton, *The Everlasting Man* (United Kingdom: Dodd, Mead, 1925), 247.
2. Ibid., 88.
3. Malcolm Muggeridge, Conversion: *The Spiritual Journey of a Twentieth-Century Pilgrim* (Eugene: Wipf and Stock Publishing, 1988), 131.
4. Huston Smith, *The World's Religions* (San Francisco: Harper, 1961), 317.
5. Ravi Zacharias, Essay from *A Slice of Infinity*, "Christianity Without Christ," February 1, 2012.
6. Paul Johnson, *History of Christianity* (United States: Touchstone, 2012), Prologue.
7. Sir William Ramsey, *The Bearing of Recent Discovery on the Trustworthiness of the New Testament*, 1915.
8. D. James Kennedy, *Why I Believe*, (Dallas: Word Publishing, 1980), 33.

Essay 9.2

9. Gregory Koukl, *The Story of Reality* (Grand Rapids: Zondervan, 2017), 101,102.
10. Gary R. Habermas, *The Verdict of History* (United Kingdom: Monarch, 1990.
11. F. F. Bruce, *The New Testament Documents: Are They Reliable?* (United Kingdom: Eerdmans Publishing Company, 2003), 123.
12. "Italian Lawyers Asked to Prove Jesus Existed," *Associated Press*, January 21, 2006.
13. Will Durant, *The Story of Civilization: Caesar and Christ, Vol 3* (New York City: Simon and Schuster, 1972), 557.
14. W.E.H. Lecky, *A History of European Morals* (London: Longmans

Green and Co. 1869), Quoted in F.F. Bruce, Jesus Lord and Savior (Downers Grove: InterVarsity Press, 1986), 15.
15. Mark Clark, *The Problem of God: Answering a Skeptic's Challenges to Christianity* (Grand Rapids: Zondervan, 2017), 87.

Essay 9.3

16. Keller, *The Reason for God,* 229, 230.
17. Lewis, *Mere Christianity,* 45.
18. C. S. Lewis, *The Grand Miracle* (New York: Ballantine Books, 1986), 113
19. Ibid., 114.

Essay 9.4

20. Herbert George Wells, "Greatest In History: Choice of Mr. H.G. Wells Christ, Buddha, and Aristotle," July 13, 1935. Launceston, Tasmania. *The Examiner,* Special Saturday Section.
21. Ibid.
22. Henry Bosch, *Encyclopedia of 7,700 Illustrations* (Rockville MD: Assurance Publishers, 1985), 647.
23. Durant, *The Story of Civilization: Caesar and Christ,* 557.
24. Ibid., 557.

Essay 9.5

25. Frank Morison, *Who Moved the Stone* (Grand Rapids: Zondervan, 1930), Preface.
26. Dallas Willard, *Renovations of the Heart* (Colorado Springs: NavPress Books, 2002), 110.
27. Gary R. Habermas, as cited in Geisler, Norman, *I Don't Have Enough Faith to Be An Atheist,* 299-300.
28. Jeffery L. Sheler, "The Last Days of Jesus," *U.S News and World Report,* April 16, 1990, 53.
29. Thomas Arnold, Christian *Life, Its Hopes, Its Fears, and Its Close,* 6th ed. (London: T. Fellowes, 1859), 15–16.

Essay 9.6

30. Philip Yancey, *The Bible Jesus Read* (Grand Rapids: Zondervan, 2002), 24.
31. Blaise Pascal, (*Pensees,* 332).
32. Peter Kreeft, *Christianity for Modern Pagans,* Ignatius Press, 1966, 264.

Essay 9.7

33. Geisler, *I Don't Have Enough Faith to Be An Atheist,* 327–329, 332, 337-338.
34. Strobel, *The Case for Christ,* 172–181.

Essay 9.8

35. Max Anders, *Holman Old Testament Commentary: Ecclesiastes, Song of Songs,* (Nashville: Holman Reference, 2004), 4.
36. Ravi Zacharias, *Jesus Among Other Gods* (Nashville: Thomas Nelson, 2000), 150.
37. Yancey, *What Good is God,* 215–216.

SECTION 10

Essay 10.1

1. Pasquini, *Atheist Persona,* 109.
2. Richard Dawkins and Steven Pinker, "Is Science Killing The Soul?" 4.7.99, chaired by Tim Radford. https://www.edge.org/conversation/is-science-killing-the-soul
3. Steven Pinker, *How the Mind Works* (United States: W. W. Norton, 2009), 146.
4. Nick Hebert, *Quantum Reality: Beyond the New Physics* (United Kingdom: Knopf Doubleday Publishing Group, 2011), 241.
5. Nicholas Humphrey, "Consciousness: The Achilles Heel of Darwinism? Thank God, Not Quite", in John Brockman (ed.), *Intelligent Thought: Science versus the Intelligent Design Movement* (Vintage, 2006), 58-9.
6. Francis Crick, *Astonishing Hypothesis: The Scientific Search for the Soul* (United Kingdom: Scribner, 1995), 3.
7. Pearcey, *Finding Truth,* 106, 107.
8. Ibid., 110.
9. Lewis Wolpert, *Six Impossible Things Before Breakfast: The Evolutionary Origins of Belief* (United Kingdom: W. W. Norton & Company, 2007), 217.
10. Flew, *There is a God,* 183.
11. Pearcey, *Finding Truth,* 109.

12. Pasquini, *Atheist Persona,* 110.
13. Geisler, *I Don't Have Enough Faith to Be An Atheist,* 139.

Essay 10.2

14. Pearcey, *Total Truth,* 211, 212.
15. Pearcey, *Saving Leonardo,* 153.
16. Pearcey, *Total Truth,* 218, 219.
17. Pearcey, *Finding Truth,* 161, 162.
18. Pearcey, *Saving Leonardo,* 152.
19. C.E.M. Joad, *The Recovery of Belief* (London, UK: Faber and Faber Limited, 1955), 16.

Essay 10.3

20. Sheldon Vanauken, *A Severe Mercy* (New York City: Harper One, 1977), 98–99.

Appendix

ISAIAH 7:14

The book of Isaiah was written in approximately 700 B.C., seven hundred years before Christ. That would be like something today written back in the 1400s pointing to an event that would occur today.

> "Therefore, the Lord Himself will give you a sign. Behold, a virgin will be with child and bear a son and she will call His name Emmanuel [which means 'God is with us']."

And the fulfillment of this prophecy you read in Matthew Chapter 1, verses 18, 24, and 25, and then in Luke 1:26-35.

MICAH CHAPTER 5, VERSE 2.

Written between 740 and 690 B.C.

> "But as for you, Bethlehem, too little to be among the clans of Judah, from you, One will go forth for Me to be ruler in Israel. His going forth are from long ago, from the days of eternity."

The prophet Micah is describing a person who is eternal, who will come into the world and be born into Bethlehem.

And it's fulfilled in Matthew 2:1 and Luke 2:4-7.

ISAIAH 9:6 (700 B.C.)

> "For a child will be born to us, a son will be given to us, and the government will rest on his shoulders and his name will be called Wonderful Counselor, Mighty God, Eternal Father, Prince of Peace."

I find it to be of great significance that this child will be called "Mighty God." Isaiah's words are a foretelling of the Incarnation, that God was going to come into the world as a human being.

And it's fulfilled in Matthew 4:15–16.

ZECHARIAH 9:9 (520 B.C.)

> "Rejoice greatly, O Daughter of Zion! Shout, daughter of Jerusalem! See, your king comes to you; righteous and having salvation, gentle and riding on a donkey, on a colt, the foal of a donkey."

And it's fulfilled in Mark 11:1–10. Take a look at what Tim Keller says in reference to this prophecy:

> "When Jesus rode into Jerusalem, people laid down their cloaks on the road in front of Him and hailed Him as a king coming in the name of the House of David. This type of parade was culturally appropriate in that era. A king would ride into town publicly and be hailed by cheering crowds, but Jesus deliberately departed from the script and did something very different. He didn't ride in on a powerful war horse the way a king would. He was mounted on a 'polos', that is, a colt or a small donkey. Here was Jesus Christ, the king of authoritative miraculous power, riding into town on a steed fit for a child or a hobbit. In this way, Jesus let it be known that He was the One prophesied in Zechariah, the great Messiah to come."

ISAIAH CHAPTER 53

The most significant of all Messianic prophecies is found in Isaiah 53.

> "Who has believed our message and to whom has the arm of the Lord been revealed? For He grew up before him like a tender shoot, And like a root out of parched ground; He has no stately form or majesty that we should look upon Him, Nor appearance that we should be attracted to Him. He was despised and forsaken of men, A man of sorrows and acquainted with grief; Surely our griefs He himself bore, And our sorrows He carried; Yet we ourselves esteemed Him stricken, smitten of God, and afflicted.
>
> But He was pierced through for our transgressions, He was crushed for our iniquities; The chastening for our well-being fell upon Him, And by His scourging we are healed. All of us like sheep have gone astray, Each of us has turned to his own way; But the Lord has caused the iniquity of us all to fall on Him. He was oppressed and He was afflicted, Yet He did not open His mouth; He was like a lamb that is led to the slaughter..."

This phrase, the "lamb that is led to the slaughter" is describing Jesus before the Roman authorities. Jesus never said a word while they were crucifying Him. He didn't even open His mouth.

> "They made his grave with the wicked, and with a rich man at his death..." (Isaiah 53:9)

We know He was crucified between two criminals and the wealthy Joseph of Arimathea buried him:

> "...because He had done no violence, nor was there any deceit in His mouth. But the Lord was pleased to crush Him, putting Him to grief; If He would render Himself as a guilt offering, He will see His offspring, He will prolong His days, and the good pleasure of the LORD will prosper in His hand. As a result of the anguish of His soul, He will see it and be satisfied; by His knowledge the Righteous One, my servant, will justify the many, and He will bear their iniquities. Therefore, I will allot Him a portion with the great, and He will divide the booty with the strong; because He poured

> out Himself to death, and was numbered with the transgressors; yet He Himself bore the sins of many, and interceded for the transgressors."

I remember speaking with a man named Baruch Maoz. He was from Boston. He grew up in the Jewish faith. Through a series of circumstances, similar to Barry Leventhal, he became a Christian and then later went to seminary and became senior pastor at one of the largest Christian churches in Israel.

I asked him this question: "How do the Jews today treat Isaiah 53? How do they deal with it? How do they explain it?"

And these were his words:

> "They treat it as if it did not exist . . . they completely ignore it."

Acknowledgments

I am first and foremost grateful to all of my family, friends, and colleagues here at The Center for Executive Leadership who have encouraged me along the way as I worked on this project. Most significantly, I want to thank Catherine Ward, Susan Wood, Susan Alison, Becky Gray and Kim Knott who have worked tirelessly to see this book become a reality.

I would be remiss if I did not acknowledge several individuals whose work has profoundly shaped my thinking and has greatly influenced the substance of this book, primarily C. S. Lewis, Tim Keller, Nancy Pearcey and Philip Yancey.

Finally, as with any writing, I acknowledge that I am standing on the shoulders of those who have come before me, with deep appreciation to the many people whose writing has informed this work.

AUTHOR CONTACT

Richard E. Simmons III welcomes inquiries and is available for speaking opportunities to groups, meetings and conferences

- For information on scheduling contact:
  Jimbo Head at jimbo@thecenterbham.org
- Email Richard at richard@richardesimmons3.com
- Visit our website at www.richardesimmons3.com

@thecenterbham @thecenterbham

@thecentertweets Richard E Simmons III

ALSO BY RICHARD E. SIMMONS III

WISDOM: LIFE'S GREAT TREASURE

Timeless Essays on the Art of Intentional Living

A collection of short essays on wisdom to serve as a guide to help people walk in wisdom on their journey towards a healthy and meaningful life.

THE TRUE MEASURE OF A MAN

How Perceptions of Success, Achievement & Recognition Fail Men in Difficult Times

In our performance-driven culture this book provides liberating truth on how to be set free from the fear of failure, comparing ourselves to others and the false ideas we have about masculinity.

ALSO BY RICHARD E. SIMMONS III

THE POWER OF A HUMBLE LIFE

Quiet Strength in an Age of Arrogance

In this book, Richard digs into the issue of pride and arrogance and then explores what he considers life's great paradox: the power of humility. The insights in this book will enable you to cultivate a humble heart so that you might experience the power of humility.

THE REASON FOR LIFE

How Perceptions of Success, Achievement & Recognition Fail Men in Difficult Times

This book seeks to help people answer the question "What is the reason for life?" by first posing a second pivotal question, which is: "Why did God put us here?" The insights in this book might enable you to understand what is the reason for life.

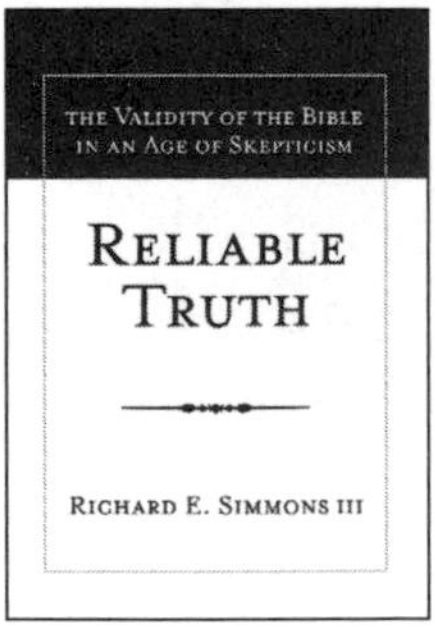

RELIABLE TRUTH

The Validity of the Bible in an Age of Skepticism

Do you believe the Bible is the inspired word of God? *Reliable Truth* offers powerful and compelling evidence why the Bible is valid and true.